CLEAR AND LIVELY WRITING

Creative Ideas and Activities, Grades 6-10

BETH MEANS
and
LINDY LINDNER

Illustrated by
Brad Lindner

1988
LIBRARIES UNLIMITED, INC.
Englewood, Colorado

LIBRARIES UNLIMITED, INC.
P.O. Box 3988
Englewood, Colorado 80155-3988

Library of Congress Cataloging-in-Publication Data

Means, Beth, 1949-
    Clear and lively writing.

    Bibliography: p. 157
    Includes index.
    1. English language--Composition and exercises
(Secondary) I. Lindner, Lindy, 1945-
II. Title.
LB1576.M434   1988   428'.007'12   88-651
ISBN 0-87287-645-4

Libraries Unlimited books are bound with Type II nonwoven material that meets and exceeds National
Association of State Textbook Administrators' Type II nonwoven material specifications Class A
through E.

To
Casey and *Ron*
for paying the phone bills

With special thanks to Marcia Olson, Anne Helmholz, Bob Cary, Dr. Nancy Pokorny, and Martha Means for patient reading and testing; Carolyn Lacey Turner, our long-suffering bird-dog on sources and errors; especially our teachers, Henriette Anne Klauser for freeing the artist within and Betty Hagman for training the craftsman; and finally, all the writers from Virgil to Gary Paulsen who wittingly or unwittingly came along for the ride.

Contents

5—EDITING WITH ENTHUSIASM (*continued*)

Foreword

Do you like living on the edge? A way with words is the way to do it. Words shape our world. What are treaties but words: written words binding nations. What is the Constitution but words: words of inspiration and direction. What is the ad for toothpaste that makes you buy, the brief in court that sends a criminal to prison, the resume that gets the job, the proposal that secures the promotion, the love letter that wins your sweetheart's affection but words; words to woo, to persuade, to entertain, to teach. A way with words is a way with life, a way to live life to its fullest, to know yourself deeply, to share yourself significantly, and a way to make a difference in our world.

Words are an interior gift as well as a gift we give to others. Power over words is power over yourself, a way to access the central core. The beauty of writing is that it taps into that part of your brain that does not know, what philosophers call "knowing without knowing": sitting down before a blank piece of paper and knowing what you want to say but not knowing how to say it. Perhaps you were trained not to begin until you knew what you were going to say; some say you cannot even start a piece until you know how it will end. I say let the writing explore the options with you. Instead of staring at a blank page, let the writing release your unknowing, the very act of writing it down frees the expression lodged in your mind. Do not wait to write until you know it all. Waiting to write until you know it all is paralyzing, because sometimes we don't know the ending before we begin, and sometimes — curious but just as true — sometimes we don't know the beginning until we come to the end. Words on paper are not meant to be a record of crystallized thought; they are the search for thought in motion, and the best writing takes the reader along on the adventure with a sense of wonder and exploration.

Writing is a process. As I would put it, it takes two halves of the brain. To make writing both fluent and fun, separate those two, using each in its respective strength at the appropriate time. Write first, then edit; that is the key to writing well and to enjoying what you write. Yet it is difficult to strike a balance. Too much emphasis on structure and form can discourage and stultify, too much freedom of expression can influence the final impact. We need heart and head — passion, yes, but passion tempered with form. How to draw the line? And where to?

These are questions that I continue to grapple with in my own work: how to harness enthusiasm and flame the pilot light of inspiration, and yet pay attention to structure and form — how to discipline and not dishearten, how to fill writers' hearts with confidence, cheerlead them on and yet challenge them to the pruning part, the part that takes the inspired ideas and respects the reader enough to present those ideas in a way that transfers the passion and the thought to an audience. And finally how to arrive at a stage where the two parts of the process meld into one, where craft and art are a seamless garment, a stage where the electrical impulses between right and left brain travel so fast and furiously as to crackle in midair with the excitement of discovery.

This gentle, encouraging, supportive book provides such a bridge. Beth Means and Lindy Lindner, real-life writer, daily life teacher, are the perfect pair to present a book about teaching writing. First, they energize and inspire you and turn you into—Superwriter! Look up in the sky! Able to dash off term papers, job resumes, love letters, and memos with a single nonstop stroke of the pen! Able to lift high spirits with words of inspiration and fervor. Able to leap over the mundane and trivial with a single bound.

Write, write, write, and keep on writing—and when you have written, do not be afraid to edit. Beth and Lindy show you how to hone your words, to carve and shape your sentences so your finished piece will have the kind of effect you want. You will be amazed at your own talent—your speed, your fluency, your impact. They will goad you and guide you. Like a good coach, these two authors challenge you to hard work, while instilling belief that you are equal to that challenge.

Who knows what power such a process will unleash? Who knows what untapped worlds you will discover and lead others to with your writing? These two gentle guides have come to support you and encourage you and give you instructions. Me? I am standing by the sidelines cheering you on. Actually, more appropriate, I am running alongside you, learning with you about my expanded world as together we explore the power of the pen. The world is waiting for your words—to amuse, to enter-tain, to persuade, to move to tears, to tickle with laughter and glee, to giggle, to cry. This book will set you on fire. It could put some danger in your life.

HENRIETTE ANNE KLAUSER, Ph.D.

Introduction: Teaching the Art and the Craft of It

Even practical day-to-day writing is both an art and a craft. It's an art because its driving force is the inspiration of the writer. It's a craft because it demands skill, patience, and practice to be done well. Your students can write better than you ever dreamed possible. They can write longer, more sustained, and livelier prose; they can edit with intelligence and enthusiasm; they can polish with care and pride. The trick is to introduce them to the art—the thrill of writing—before you gently guide them into learning the craft of it.

One of the delights of writing is that professionals and novices share the same problems. Everyone who writes is a writer. Many of the tricks that help the published author also help the novice. To write this book, one writer and one teacher got together and asked both teachers and students what they would like to know. We then searched the literature for pieces by writers on writing and talked to writers about how they work. Like squirrels in fall, we gathered nuggets that we thought would help novice writers and tried them in our workshops. If they helped at least some of the students improve their writing, we put them in the book. Although the book is written for middle and high school teachers, once students get past the point where forming the letters with a pen consumes all of their attention, there isn't much difference between teaching youngsters and adults. Most adults enjoy doing the classroom activities as personal exercises to improve their writing.

The book is organized around "the writing process" which breaks the long business of writing into three common-sense steps:

1. Get a clear idea of what you are going to write about (prewriting).

2. Get the words on paper (drafting).

3. Adjust it (editing).

As school systems put more emphasis on writing, many are adopting the writing process as their basic method of teaching writing from first through twelfth grades—to the great benefit of students. In this book, we try to provide middle school and early high school teachers with practical classroom activities and the technical information they need to teach writing as a process.

The first two chapters cover prewriting activities from getting ideas to making outlines, along with a few basic terms to help students discuss their plans. The third chapter covers the all-important work of getting words on paper, while the fourth chapter presents some specific writing techniques, such as writing examples or dialogue. The last chapter covers explaining and managing the editing process, along with a few tips on publishing student pieces. Sprinkled throughout the chapters are sections with tips and comments on teaching titled "Teacher's Notebook" and professional tips that may help student writers called "Notes from the Pros."

Because we believe that all writing is creative, we chose simple classroom activities that can be easily adapted to writing projects in all classes: science, social studies, and business as well as English and so-called "creative writing" classes. Youngsters learn as much about writing in these other subjects as they do in English class. Teachers in these fields need, if anything, more ideas on how to help students write than do the specialists. In order to make it easier for those who are not writing or language arts teachers to adapt our activities to their subjects, we have written the activity instructions as we give them to our writing students. With writing, sometimes simple explanations are what teachers need most.

When teachers begin to teach writing as a process, they soon discover that they not only need to adapt their classroom activities but they also must revamp their writing assignments. The traditional "report" or "paper" on a specified topic is out because the writing process begins with learning to develop and choose one's own topics. Furthermore, vague types (or *genres* as we prefer to call them) of writing like the "report" or "essay" are among the most difficult to write. Children first need plenty of practice with the simpler genres, such as "how-to's," "ten tips," and fiction.

While the change may be disconcerting to teachers trained only to write "papers" themselves, it makes good sense. A beginning writer faced with both an unfamiliar subject and an unfamiliar genre is like a beginning driver faced with a Los Angeles freeway. There are too many things to learn at once. It is much easier to teach youngsters the basics of writing with topics they choose themselves, using simple genres. The initial spark of enthusiasm that comes from choosing a subject of interest to the writer, along with the comfort of working in a more familiar genre, are essential to developing enough enthusiasm and self-confidence to carry students through the long writing process.

Each new genre they tackle teaches students something more about writing. They will learn more about writing for an audience by writing a how-to than any other format. Nothing teaches young writers that they must make sense to a reader than writing fiction. Opinion pieces and film critiques teach students how to mount an argument. "Ten Tips for Keeping Your Parents Happy" not only teaches the young writer something about parents but also something about structure and design in writing. Writing an adventure story or historical romance requires as much knowledge of geography or history as does a paper on India or the American Revolution. When their stories fall apart for lack of characterization or plot, they learn as much about planning as they do from writing outlines.

When students learn to revise and polish any type of writing, they learn a little more about writing technique. They also learn that not everything they try turns out. As long as they keep writing with enthusiasm, they will learn the most important lesson on writing—to persevere.

Teaching writing to a classroom of bouncing thirteen-year-olds or bored sixteen-year-olds is not easy. Just the amount of time it consumes is a problem. Teaching students to write fluently and confidently by the time they leave for college or a job requires almost daily practice through middle school and high school. But what students learn about the art and craft of writing in middle school and high school will affect their opportunities for schooling, jobs, and self-expression for the rest of their lives. We salute every teacher who troubles over it and hope every one of them finds something in this book to help them.

Chapter 1

Deciding What to Write About

CHAPTER CONTENTS

Waiting for inspiration is like waiting for friends. If you sit around the house and don't go out and meet them, they will never come. You have to make things happen. Writing is an active occupation, not a passive one.

— Judy Delton

INTRODUCTION

Like many adults, youngsters often think their own lives too dull to write about. Writers must be special people — minor gods who drop books into the library by magic. "Did your hair freeze off when you were in the Arctic?" one of our students seriously asked an author, apparently surprised that a writer, like a parent or a teacher, could be bald.

Ask published writers where their ideas came from and, time and again, they will point to some small incident in everyday life that they simply enlarged or to something they read in the newspaper or a book. Marcel Proust got the ideas for the Swann stories while dipping a cookie in a cup of tea. Agatha Christie claimed that her best ideas came while doing the dishes. They discovered writing when they discovered that they didn't need to lead a special life to write.

Students need to know that those stories and books they see in the library are the creations of ordinary people like themselves. Even the simplest life is rich with starting points for writing. The details that make fiction sing and nonfiction concrete come from the commonplace world that surrounds each of us. Because no two people lead the same life or see life the same way, each person's writing is indeed special. The writing club is open to everyone. All one needs to join is an idea or two to write about.

The Writing Idea Triangle

The first task of the writer is to choose what to write about, that is, to find a specific writing idea. It is a bit difficult to explain exactly what makes a good writing idea, so it helps students to think of a writing idea as a triangle (see the illustration on p. 4).

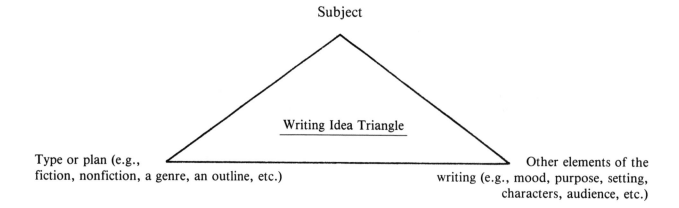

Any point of the triangle can serve as a starting point, but two points and usually all three are needed to make a writing idea. For example, any subject can serve as a jumping-off point for an infinite number of writing ideas. The subject may be horses, but the writing idea needs something more:

a character: a story about a horse named Looney Tune

a setting: a story about a horse ranch

an explanation: how to groom a horse

an opinion: why I don't like horses

a question: what was the economic importance of horses to the nineteenth century?

a design: descriptions of horse breeds arranged alphabetically by name

The writing idea may come from the type of writing. When we asked a group of students who were studying the ancient Egyptians for writing ideas about the pyramids, they came up with:

a story: a day in the life of an Egyptian pyramid-builder

a how-to: how to build a pyramid

an explanation: why the Egyptians built pyramids

tips: five problems with building a pyramid in your backyard

Even a very closely defined topic is just a starting point for finding writing ideas. Why did Hannibal fail as a military leader?

Hannibal failed because he ran out of money.

Hannibal failed because he was too far from home.

Hannibal failed because his men didn't like him.

Who can forget Will Cuppy's wonderful idea: Hannibal failed because he refused to admit that elephants always run backwards in the face of enemy fire.

We explain to students that they need to find a writing idea before they write anything, except for a personal journal entry, because a story or a nonfiction piece is not just a collection of paragraphs, it's a collection of paragraphs unified by one idea. This central idea distinguishes a scrawl from a story and one story from another. It describes what a piece is about and ties it into a unified whole.

Our rule is that a teacher or a publisher may assign the starting point, but finding the writing idea is *always* the responsibility of the writer. This rule not only helps students narrow their topics, it also gives them some stake in their writing. Enthusiasm is an indispensable tool of the writer. A sense of choice and responsibility is essential to enthusiasm. We have another, equally important rule we tell our students: Don't sit around waiting for writing ideas to come to you. Go out and find them!

FINDING YOUR OWN STARTING POINTS

This chapter is divided into two main sections. The first has activities to help students find starting points for writing—principally subjects—in the world around them. The activities in the second half show students how to take starting points and convert them into writing ideas by adding other writing elements or by choosing a type of writing.

Activity 1:
Stop, Look, and Listen

There is only one trait that marks the writer. He is always watching. It's a kind of trick of mind he is born with.

—Morley Callaghan

The beauty of "Stop, Look, and Listen" is its simplicity. Anyone can do it in a minute or two. Students can use it at school, at home, on field trips, or on vacation.

Instructions to Students

Stop, get out a piece of paper or your writing ideas notebook (see "Teacher's Notebook: On Keeping a Writing Ideas Notebook," p. 11), and write down ten things you see and ten things you hear. Don't be picky. Anything will do. Work quickly. It shouldn't take you more than a minute.

Once you finish the list, pick a few items. See if they suggest any writing ideas or questions that might become writing ideas. Note the writing ideas at the bottom of the page and mark them clearly, so you can find them later on.

EXAMPLE

Starting Point—Stop, Look, and Listen List (made while sitting in a classroom after school one day)

	SEE		HEAR
1.	desk	1.	lawn mower
2.	tennis shoes	2.	freeway noise
3.	picture of an Amazonian frog	3.	pages ruffling
4.	grass	4.	siren
5.	pencil	5.	computer printer
6.	sink	6.	"Who put the coffee grounds in the sink?"
7.	computer	7.	"This school is a mess."
8.	glasses	8.	giggling girls
9.	hand	9.	whack, whack of library cart

Writing Ideas

Desk. Why do they make those little half desks instead of full ones? Is it to cram more kids in a class like passengers on a no-frills airline? Who thought up the idea? This might make an interesting research piece or a good funny piece speculating on all the crazy reasons.

This school is a mess. Interview the school janitors to find out their problems with keeping the school clean, perhaps writing a list of ways students and teachers could help out. Write a science paper on the chemicals in cleaning products.

Glasses. Visit a local optometrist to find out how glasses are made, how optometrists are trained, or why people decide to become optometrists. Write a funny poem explaining why glasses get sat on. Write a paper for health class on how glasses help people see.

Additional Notes to Teachers

There are many ways to use stop, look, and listen lists. Try some of these variations on the theme for fun.

1. Make the lists in specific places, such as a museum, an airport, a train, a plane, in a classroom decorated to reflect a subject, on any field trip, or in a favorite place.

2. Make the lists at specific times, such as during a film or television show, a classroom activity or laboratory period, during school assembly, just before bedtime or early in the morning, once during vacation, or every day at 4:35 p.m.

3. Make the lists in response to any interesting piece of art, music, dance, or photography.

4. Add "ten things you think" to "ten things you see and hear."

5. If you have the luxury of cameras and tape recorders, by all means take pictures or make tape recordings of the items on the lists. The pictures and tapes can be used to inspire writing or to illustrate final products.

6. Try limiting the list to specific types of starting points. Art teachers may want only things of a certain size or color. Science teachers can limit the list to things expressing certain principles of physics, chemistry, or math. Music teachers can limit the list to soft sounds, rhythmic sounds, or sounds expressing a particular mood.

Activity 2:
This Is Your Life

Writing comes more easily if you have something to say.
—Sholem Asch

There is an old rule among writers: "When you are learning to write, first write about yourself, the things you know, and your own experiences." It's still a good rule. We like to use starting points from "This Is Your Life" for assignments focused on practicing technique rather than content.

Students enjoy this activity and often want to keep writing, expanding their answers. Be sure to plan time to let them strike while the inspiration is hot in addition to collecting starting points and writing ideas for the future.

Because there are so few books on writing for students this age, we use handouts extensively. Writing takes so much time that students often need to finish up at home and the handouts make good reminders. Instead of handouts, you can leave the questions or reminders on the blackboard or on an overhead projection while students work.

Instructions to Students

Write your answers to the questions on the "This Is Your Life" handout. This is *not* a test. We ask your opinions about many things. Answer honestly. We also ask you to remember events. If you can't remember, close your eyes and think a minute, then write down the first answer that comes to you. If you still can't think of anything, make up an imaginary answer. When you are finished, go over your answers and find at least three starting points. Note any writing ideas as well. Select any answer and write about it for a few minutes.

THIS IS YOUR LIFE (HANDOUT)

1. Write down anything in your life you would like to write about.

2. Name your favorite food.

3. Name the food you hate the most.

4. Name three things you like to do. Why do you like doing them?

5. Name three things you hate doing. Why do you hate doing them?

6. Name two places you especially like to be. Why do you like being there?

7. Name two places you dislike being. Why do you dislike being there?

8. If you could do anything you wanted, what would you do?

9. Name two things you have never done but would like to try.

10. What is the best thing you've ever done?

11. What is the worst thing you've ever done?

12. What is the funniest thing you've ever done?

13. Do you own a pet? If so, list some of the things your pet does.

14. Name your brothers and sisters. List some of the best, worst, or funniest things they have ever done.

15. Name two things that scare you.

16. Name two things that make you happy.

17. If you were in charge of the world, name three changes you would make.

18. What is your first memory?

19. List any five things you know.

20. List any five things you don't know.

21. What is your favorite book? What is the best part?

22. Now go back and answer the first question again.

23. Make up a question about your life and answer it.

Activity 3:
Borrowing Lists

Research is to see what everybody else has seen,
and to think what nobody else has thought.
— Albert Szen-Gyorgyi

This activity is an excellent introduction to the reference section of the library as well as a good way to find starting points.

Instructions to Students

Let any book fall open to a page and write down five words, facts, or opinions on that page. You can also let it fall open to five different pages. Some books are especially interesting. Try using at least one of the books we mention and find one of your own. If you can't find them, ask the school library media specialist for help. Look for:

- *Dictionaries*: Any word in a dictionary can become a starting point. Special dictionaries are also intriguing. A good example is *Morris Dictionary of Word and Phrase Origins: Vols. 1, 2, 3* by William and Mary Morris. It is full of fascinating information. For example, the word *motel* was invented by an architect in San Luis Obispo, California, in 1925. Although *kid* means a young goat, it has been used as an affectionate name for children since Shakespeare's time. According to H. L. Mencken's *The American Language*, another useful reference, *kid* is used in American English for *co-pilot*. Try subject dictionaries. Dictionaries on science, art, music, law, computers, writing, and publishing can be found in most libraries. *The People's Chronology: A Year-by-Year Record of Human Events from Prehistory to the Present*, edited by James Trager, is wonderful for historical starting points. Try *What's What*, a dictionary of pictures with the correct names for things like venetian blinds.

- *Encyclopedias*: Try short encyclopedias, such as *The New American Desk Encyclopedia* (1984) from Signet's New American Library, or use books of lists instead, such as Irving Wallace's *The Book of Lists*, Isaac Asimov's *Book of Facts*, and the International Reading Association's *The Teacher's Book of Lists*.

- *Quotation Books*: Books or quotations provide good starting points for writing. Most people think of Bartlett's *Familiar Quotations*, but quotation books arranged by subject are often more interesting. Good examples are the *Dictionary of Quotations* by Bergen Evans, the *International Thesaurus of Quotations* by Rhoda Thomas Tripp, and *Peter's Quotations: Ideas for Our Time* by Laurence J. Peter. There are also many books of quotations on particular subjects.

Notes from the Pros:
On the Principle of Creativity

In *The Performing Flea*, P. G. Wodehouse notes that the best story ideas almost always sound ridiculous and illustrates his point with a delightfully absurd "writing idea" version of *Hamlet*, beginning "See, there was this guy...."

When your students first begin to record ideas, be sure to stress writing down the starting points or ideas before they make *any* decisions about them. This rule also applies to rough drafts. Creativity is not killed by judging if something is brilliant or mundane, serious or silly, good or bad: all creations are subject to judgments eventually. Creativity is killed by judging too soon.

Teacher's Notebook: On Personal,
Practice, and Portfolio Assignments

To increase the amount of practice students receive without increasing the paper storm that always accompanies writing assignments, have students keep all rough drafts in a "Personal Journal" or a "Practice Journal" and all polished pieces in a "Portfolio." Students share their personal journal entries only when they wish; practice journals are turned in by a few students each week; polished pieces go in a student's portfolio. This little system not only keeps papers from flying around and reduces numbers of papers the teacher must read, it encourages students to keep their writing, even their unedited writing, over a long period of time. P. G. Wodehouse points out that success in writing comes so gradually that writers are always surprised at their progress when they look back. If students toss out their assignments, they never have the chance to see their progress.

There are always a few students in every group who discover the joy of writing through the personal journal. Some students have trouble writing because they worry too much about the teacher's expectations and as a result write correct but dull pieces. Others are convinced that they haven't much imagination and need the luxury of a personal journal before they will attempt fiction or poetry. Those with poor self-esteem often gain enthusiasm and confidence through personal journal entries that they gain no other way. Knowing that they needn't show failures to anyone helps this group separate writing and editing—or the expectation of editing. This improves their fluency and makes writing less painful.

The practice journal is the most important—and overlooked—learning tool for the novice writer. Curiously, people expect young violinists to squeak away in practice and young golfers to muff shot after shot at the driving range, but they forget that young writers also need the same kind of small-scale practice and plenty of stray practice shots. Young musicians are also taught to isolate small sections of a work and practice the section over and over, whereas young writers are rarely told to practice an isolated paragraph of dialogue, a description, or a conclusion several times. By keeping all their rough drafts and their practice paragraphs in a journal, students learn to practice writing properly, to expect a certain amount of failure, to keep practicing, and to edit their work before they share it outside of their writing group. A quick scan through a practice journal gives the teacher a much better sense of a student's progress, attitude, and problems than one paper in a pile.

All novice writers must learn to revise and polish a draft into a quality piece of which they are truly proud. In our experience, students get more out of polishing one *C* piece into an *A* piece than by turning in five different *C* pieces, so we limit the number of portfolio assignments and set fairly strong standards that the piece must achieve before it can be put in the portfolio. To encourage students to edit, we give them the chance to edit and reedit any piece until it meets portfolio standards and hold a little class celebration any time a student gets a piece into the portfolio. Writing is hard work; they deserve the applause. This reduces the time students waste typing, freeing up time for practice or revision.

We also recommend basing the grading system on the personal, practice, and portfolio assignments (see "Teacher's Notebook: On Grading Papers," p. 136).

Teacher's Notebook: On Keeping a Writing Ideas Notebook

Nothing is more reassuring than a pocketful of starting points and writing ideas. We ask our students to keep a "Starting Points and Writing Ideas Notebook" for writing assignments or for writing in their personal journals. The results of the activities in this chapter and ideas they find themselves go in the notebook. A 3-by-5-inch spiralbound notebook is ideal because students can carry it wherever they go. Some students enjoy keeping their writing ideas notebook cross-referenced on a computer database.

CONVERTING STARTING POINTS INTO WRITING IDEAS

The trick to finding good writing ideas is to look for many ideas and then choose the best. The activities in the rest of this chapter show students how to develop many writing ideas from any one starting point. The activities should be played like games. The object is to come up with several writing ideas, no matter how dull or silly they sound at first. One can usually find a very good idea on any list of four or five. Most of the activities can be done alone, in small groups, or as a class.

Activity 4: The Three-Minute Fastwrite

Just as appetite comes by eating, so work brings inspiration,
if inspiration is not discernible at the beginning.
— Igor Stravinsky

Three minutes of concentrated writing is an amazing amount of time to a writer. A person's first thoughts on a starting point are often the most original and powerful ones. Simply writing down first thoughts for three minutes is one of the easiest ways to generate the best writing ideas. The first time you introduce fastwriting, be sure to choose very simple starting points. We like "breakfast," "the best time of the day," and "school."

Instructions to Students

Get out your practice journal or a piece of paper and a comfortable pen. When you fastwrite, always use pens that feel comfortable in your hand and which flow freely. To do this exercise, write as fast as you can for three minutes about a starting point.

Don't try to write well. Just write the first things that come to mind. Don't cross out. If you change your mind, add the change in the margin or at the bottom of the page. We are going to use the three-minute fastwrite all year, so this first time, you are going to practice. We'll assign a starting point, turn over our three-minute egg-timer, and tell you to go. At the end of three minutes, we'll assign another starting point. Ready? The first starting point is breakfast. Go....

Read through your fastwrites and note any writing ideas you have at the bottom of the page.

Additional Notes to Teachers

The three-minute fastwrite has plenty of uses, both in writing classrooms and elsewhere. It can be used as:

- a daily fluency exercise.

- a way to get students started on a new assignment.

- a way to consolidate students' understanding of a lesson.

- a pause in the middle of a social studies class or a science class to help students learn the subject; room can be found in the busiest week for three minutes every few days.

- a "sponge" activity to open or close out a lesson.

Activity 5:
Fiction, Nonfiction, or Poetry?

Nonfiction is saying, "I caught a 12-inch fish." Fiction is saying, "I caught the biggest trout I ever saw before." In a lot of ways, fiction is more true than nonfiction.

—Gary Paulsen

Unlike botanists, writers have never organized their terminology into consistent classes, families, and species. Until they do, it's easiest to introduce students to different types of writing with the following simple definitions of fiction, nonfiction, and poetry:

- *Fiction*: Written works based on the writer's imagination. Fiction includes short stories, novels, plays, and any other piece of writing, except poems, in which the people, places, and events of the story are created from the writer's imagination. The imaginary people in fiction are called *characters*, and the imaginary places are called *settings*. The imaginary events of a story make up the *plot*.

- *Nonfiction*: Written works based on either facts or opinions. Nonfiction is the biggest category of writing. Nonfiction includes essays, opinion pieces, magazine articles of all kinds, letters, histories, biographies, and even cookbooks and dictionaries. Almost everything that is neither fiction nor poetry is nonfiction.

- *Poetry*: Poetry is the most personal of all writing. Poet A. E. Housman said "I could no more define poetry than a terrier can define a rat." But a terrier knows a rat when it sees one, and most people recognize a poem when they see one. A piece is a poem because the writer says it's a poem. Poetry is not writing that rhymes, although some poems do rhyme.

Instructions to Students

Choose any starting point and write down a fiction, nonfiction, and poetry idea for each. Writing ideas often come to mind in fiction or nonfiction form. Choosing one of the three categories is an easy way to turn a starting point into a writing idea.

EXAMPLE

Starting Point — A paragraph from the "This Is Your Life" activity about a blind dog named Alice

"Alice is blind. She carries her bowl around in her mouth when she wants food. She comes to work with me. Sometimes she waits in the shower or stands on my shoes in the morning when she wants me to hurry. She also snores. She can find her way out of any yard or building. The worst thing she ever did was dump a gallon-bottle of cooking oil on the living room rug."

Writing Ideas

Fiction: "My Dog Wears Purple Tennis Shoes," a story about Alice getting ready for work.
Nonfiction: How to care for a blind dog.
Poetry: A poem based on my feelings when Alice went blind.

Activity 6:
The Genre Game

An idea is a feat of association.
—Robert Frost

The genre game is a student favorite. The word *genre* comes from the French word for *type*. It refers to similar pieces of writing. Used mainly to refer to fiction, it applies to nonfiction as well.

There are hundreds of genres. Be sure to explain to students that genres are not precise types. Genres develop because writers like a particular writer's work and use some of the ideas in their own work. For example, the mystery genre was inspired by Wilkie Collins's novel *The Moonstone* and Sir Arthur Conan Doyle's Sherlock Holmes stories. So many writers have used this genre since then that subgenres ("the detective mystery," "the English mystery," the "adventure-mystery") are now developing. On the nonfiction side, the essay is the invention of one man, Michel de Montaigne, a seventeenth-century lawyer and eccentric who retired to a real ivy-covered tower to write his *Essays*.

The word *essayer* means *to try* in French. Montaigne's notion was to use each essay to try one idea or one theme. Since then, the formal essay, the informal essay, the personal essay, the general academic essay, and specialized academic essays have developed as subgenres.

Instructions to Students

Review the handout with the starter list of genres. Write down one writing idea for every genre. Don't worry about how good the ideas are, just try to come up with something. If you don't know very much about the starting point, it helps to write down the few things you do know before playing the game. When you are finished, put a checkmark next to the ideas you like best.

STARTER LIST OF GENRES (HANDOUT)

POPULAR FICTION GENRES

Nostalgia:	Stories based on memories of a character's past.
Tall Tale:	Exaggerated accounts of a real or imagined event.
Mystery:	Stories about solving a mystery.
Romance:	Stories about falling into or out of love.
Choose your own ending:	Stories written like a computer game where the reader chooses which paragraphs to read.
Adventure:	Stories showing characters overcoming danger.
Science fiction:	Stories set on imaginary planets, in imaginary societies, or in the future.
Fantasy:	Stories set in imaginary kingdoms or stories about mythical beasts or characters with special powers.
Horror:	Scary stories.
Historical fiction:	Stories set in the real historical past with imaginary characters or plots.

POPULAR NONFICTION GENRES

Nostalgia:	Pieces based on memories of the writer.
Personal experience:	Pieces based on an event or problem in the lives of real people.
How-to:	Explanations of how to build, make, or operate things.
Self-help:	Pieces similar to how-to pieces, but based on helping people overcome personal problems like getting good grades or making friends. Self-help pieces don't emphasize step-by-step instructions as much as how-to's do.
Profile:	Pieces about an interesting person or group of people.
Consumer:	Tips on buying, selling, or repairing.
Opinion:	Pieces in which the writer expresses an opinion and makes a case for his or her point of view.
Information:	Straightforward presentations of facts new to the reader.
History:	Pieces which explain the history of people, places, things, or ideas.
Reporting:	Newspaper-style explanations of current events.
Collection:	Collections of almost anything; for example, a dictionary is a collection of word definitions and spellings. A cookbook is a collection of recipes.
Biography:	Life stories of interesting people.
Autobiography:	The life story of the writer.
Essay:	Pieces presenting, explaining, or arguing for one idea or theme. Subgenres are informal (often humorous), formal, personal, and academic.

POETRY

There are only a few genres of poems; for example, haiku or sonnets. Usually the poet wants to write a poem that is one of a kind, not part of a genre. Poems can be based on memories, moods, observations, feelings, impressions, ideas, rhyme or rhythm.

To play the genre game, write the names of the fiction and nonfiction genres down the left-hand side of the page along with a list of the things which inspire poems. Then write your writing ideas for each one down the right-hand side of the page.

EXAMPLE

Starting Point—Amazonian frog (from "Stop, Look, and Listen List," p. 6)

Writing Ideas

FICTION GENRES

Nostalgia:	*Summer of the Amazon*, a story of a boy's summer in the Amazon River Basin.
Tall Tale:	Story of a dinner where the guests are served frog legs to their distress. Title: *The Great Frog Leg Rebellion.*
Mystery:	Murder mystery where poison from an Amazonian frog skin is used as the murder weapon.
Romance:	Story of a biologist who falls in love with a woman reporter who has come to write an article on his work.
Choose your own ending:	Your spaceship has crashed on THE FROG PLANET (oops). What do you do next?
Adventure:	Tale of a fishing trip to Brazil that goes awry when one of the party tries to catch a frog.
Science fiction:	Life on a jungle planet.
Fantasy:	A story about a little boy whose pet frog can tell him the future.
Horror:	A story in which weird things happen every time the frogs start croaking.
Historical fiction:	A story set in Brazil at the turn of the century.

NONFICTION GENRES

Nostalgia:	Memories of my father reading stories about places like the Amazon and dreaming of going there.
Personal experience:	Frogs in the basement, a true tale.
How-to:	How to study frog anatomy.
Self-help:	Overcome your fear of frogs.

Profile: *The Man Who Loves Frogs*: story of a biologist who studies Amazonian frogs.

Consumer: Importing frogs is illegal! Ten tips to help consumers avoid buying endangered species.

Opinion: Why we should protect rare species.

Information: How the Indians of the Amazon live.

History: History of the discovery of a rare species in the Amazon.

Reporting: Reporting on the biology class study project on Amazonian frogs.

Collection: Collection of class frog stories and articles.

Biography: Biography of the first anthropologist to work among the Amazonian Indians.

Autobiography: Why I have never been interested in frogs.

Essay: Comparing Amazonian frogs to North American frogs.

POETRY

memories: My father's voice reading Amazon tales.

observations: A poem called "Night Sounds."

feelings: My feelings when I read about faraway Brazil and frogs.

impressions: Impressions of a classroom with an Amazonian frog picture on the wall.

ideas: Even something as ugly as a frog can inspire us.

Activity 7:
Who, What, Why, When, Where, and How

I keep six honest serving men
(They taught me all I knew)
Their names are What and Why and When
And How and Where and Who.
     —Rudyard Kipling

Following a simple, structured procedure can bring ideas to mind by giving one's imagination a little push to get going on its own. This exercise is especially useful for nonfiction ideas. We like to use it on Friday afternoon when the class is too tired to feel very imaginative.

Instructions to Students

Get out your writing ideas notebook. Write down your starting point at the top of the page. Then write down a question about your starting point beginning with who, what, why, when, where, or how. Look at the question and try to write down two more questions or comments about your question.

Go back to your starting point and do the same thing over again. If you used what to write your first question, use who, why, when, where, or how for your next questions. Keep going until you have at least one question beginning with who, one beginning with what, and so forth. Note any writing ideas at the bottom of the page. Silly questions are permitted.

EXAMPLE

Starting Point—freeway noise (from a stop, look, and listen list)

Questions

Where does the noise come from? the wheels or the car engines? bumps on the surface of the road?

What have people been doing to reduce noise from freeways? building fences? planting trees? tearing down old roads?

How does noise affect people? Does it make them sick? Can too much noise ruin your hearing? How much is too much?

When is it noisiest? at night? rush hour? last day of school?

Who studies noise? engineers? doctors? who else?

Why does noise exist? What makes sound? What stops sound? Is there any sound in space?

Writing Ideas

A research story about whether or not there is any sound in space.
An article on how noise affects people and animals.

EXAMPLE

Starting Point—a pencil (from a stop, look, and listen list)

Questions

How do they get the lead to go down the middle of the pencil? It's such a tight fit, you would think it grew that way. Do they have special machines to drill the holes?

When you plant a used pencil in the ground, will a new pencil grow? Do the pencil makers plant pencil seeds to grow new pencils?

Where are the pencil forests? Do they use leftover trees or big newly cut trees to make pencils? Maybe they glue scraps of wood together.

What kind of trees make the best pencils? fir trees? pine trees? hardwoods?

Why do pencils always break or disappear just as you start to take a test or a phone message? Does somebody train them, or is it a pencil instinct? How come you never throw pencils away, but they never seem to be around when you need them? Where do they go?

Who invented the pencil? What inspired the inventor? Did the same person invent the pen?

Writing Ideas

The history of the lowly pencil.
A humorous essay called "The Truth about Pencils."
An information piece explaining how pencils are made.

Activity 8:
People, Places, and Problems

Whatever pulls you to it like a secret magnet may be your story meat. Your imagination is a mysterious and somewhat holy place.

—Paul Darcy Boles

This exercise is the fiction equivalent of who, what, why, when, where, and how. It is based on arbitrarily inventing a character, a setting, and a problem for the character to solve.

Instructions to Students

Set up a piece of paper with four headings across the top: *Starting Point, Person (Character), Place (or Setting),* and *Problem (or Central Conflict).* To play the game, think up a starting point, person, a place, and a problem that person wants or needs to solve. You can use a starting point to suggest people, places, or problems, or you can just make them up. Give the person a name, if you haven't already. Then write, "This is a story about a _____, named _____, who _____
_____. Just fill in the blanks.

EXAMPLE

Starting Point	*Person*	*Place*	*Problem*
desk	a boy	sitting at desk	lost homework

This is a story about a boy, named Jim, who is always losing his assignments and has just discovered that he has lost his social studies homework for the third time in a row....

EXAMPLE

Starting Point	*Person*	*Place*	*Problem*
siren	elderly lady	house near hospital	hates sirens

This is a story about an elderly lady, named Florence, who lived in London during the Blitz and can't stand sirens....

EXAMPLE

Starting Point	*Person*	*Place*	*Problem*
pages ruffling	librarian	sailboat	bored

This is a story about a librarian, named Jack, who is bored with his job and wants adventure. One day on his way to work, he is attracted by an advertisement seeking a cook for a sailboat going on a race around the world....

EXAMPLE

Starting Point	*Person*	*Place*	*Problem*
"This school is a mess"	girl	Planet Xenon	a tidy person on a messy planet

This is a story about a student, named Jeso, who goes away to school on the planet Xenon and is disgusted that the school—and everything else—is a mess because Xenonites don't care about litter. So she goes on a crusade to change their ways....

Activity 9:
Wacko

What happens to the hole when the cheese is gone?
—Bertolt Brecht

Wacko is so named because the wackier your mood, the more fun it is. Frankly, we like playing Wacko with students even when they aren't looking for writing ideas. This is a great group game that calls for a certain amount of inspired lunacy.

Instructions to Students

Get out your writing ideas notebook. Choose an item from any of your lists that is a fact, an opinion, or an observation. Then make it go wacko by turning the idea upside down or changing it around. Let your first wacky idea lead to others and keep going until you run dry. One of your wacky ideas just might turn out to be a good writing idea.

EXAMPLE

Starting Point—"I hate zucchini" (from the "This Is Your Life" activity)

Wacky Ideas

Suppose I like zucchini. Suppose zucchini liked me! Could zucchinis be trying to get my attention? Is that why they grow to forty pounds overnight if I fail to pick them each evening? Is that why zucchinis appear on my doorstep or my desk when I'm not looking?

Writing Idea

A silly story called *The Zucchini Conspiracy* about what zucchinis really do when people aren't looking.

EXAMPLE

Starting Point—"From all levels of government, federal, state, and local, Americans get 150,000 new laws and 2 million new regulations every year." (Isaac Asimov, *Book of Facts*, p. 197)

Wacky Ideas

Suppose a country could only pass one law each year. What law would people choose? Most people would probably choose "love thy neighbor" as the best law. Would it work? Maybe not.

Writing Idea

A fictional newspaper article like this one from *The National Snoop* (Anywhere, U.S.A.)

Mr. Jake Blunt, owner of the Flat Earth Deli and Gas station, was hauled into Superior Court today and charged with two counts of Not Loving Thy Neighbor. Blunt allegedly snarled at his neighbor on two separate occasions for not returning Blunt's lawnmower. Blunt was found guilty on both counts and paid a $100.00 fine.

"There otta be a law," growled Blunt at reporters afterwards. Reporters reminded him there was a law: "Love thy neighbor."

"Yeah?" replied Blunt. "Well it's not all it's cracked up to be."

Additional Notes to Teachers

Be sure to remind students that sometimes ideas come to mind in whole paragraphs and stories. Tell them to get it on paper while the inspiration is hot.

Notes from the Pros:
On Falling in Love and Burning Out

Writing begins with passion: passion for the subject; passion for the genre; passion for the ideas. Passion is the engine that drives writing. Without it, writers cannot sustain the energy to finish. Writers who work on contracts specifying the same genres and the same subjects over and over burn out. Sir Arthur Conan Doyle killed Sherlock Holmes just to escape from the genre and the character. Other writers have stopped writing altogether. The wise ones went back to the beginning and started with a genre and a theme of their own choosing—with a passion.

Students don't begin to really learn to write until they fall in love with a story, a genre, a subject, or an idea and write about it with all their heart. It's a great moment. Unfortunately, most students never discover it because school curriculums often have the process backwards. Students are assigned "papers" on specified topics over and over and over. They burn out before they ever fall in love.

If you want to turn your students on to writing, remember that passion comes first. Let them choose what to write about and how to write it over and over. Don't save creative writing for the best students. Creative writing *is* writing; the worst students need to discover that passion before they will improve. Keep moving on, so that students can try new genres, new subjects, and new ideas. Teach them terms and techniques one day; leave them to write without direction the next. Do some practice pieces, some complete pieces. Above all, avoid the burnout assignment. Then wait patiently for them to fall in love.

Teacher's Notebook: On Genres

The essay is the most difficult genre to write and to teach. The other nonfiction genres are good alternatives for younger students, who may not yet have developed a sufficient grip on abstract thinking processes to manage an essay, and for students who are having trouble with organization.

To help students with nonfiction, start them on genres based on chronology: fiction, how-to's, personal experience, and nostalgia. Once they are writing more clearly, try genres with simple patterns, such as lists (ten tips on anything, five ways to do anything), question and answer interviews, and collections. The sections of these pieces can be cut apart later and rearranged into nonchronological patterns such as "most important to least important," "comparison and contrast," "general to specific," etc. Finally, help students explore cause and effect through character motivation, planting clues in mysteries, foreshadowing events, and planning choose-your-own-ending stories. Students who have had success with fiction and the easier nonfiction genres are much better prepared to handle rhetorical writing later on.

With all the nonfiction genres, it helps students to see several good examples of the genre before they attempt it on their own. Except for essays, examples are easy to find in almost every popular magazine. Don't overlook magazines like *Popular Mechanics*, *Consumer Reports*, or specialty magazines on sports or hobbies.

You'll have better luck with the essay itself if you start student on informal, humorous essays and work up to formal essays. Finding essay examples for younger students is extremely difficult. The best collection of essays we've found is *The Bedford Reader* by X. J. Kennedy and Dorothy Kennedy. Although most of the essays are too difficult for students younger than about fifteen or sixteen, you can read abridged excerpts or some of the simpler ones aloud to younger students. Try *Merlyn's Pen*, a writing magazine for middle school and high school students, or the Pat McManus stories from *A Fine and Pleasant Misery* or *They Shoot Canoes, Don't They?* for informal, humorous essays that youngsters like.

Chapter 2

Planning

CHAPTER CONTENTS

*Plans will get you into things
but you got to work your way out.*
—Will Rogers

INTRODUCTION

When most people think of writing plans, they think of an outline. English teachers faithfully teach the outline and usually ask students to turn it in with the finished piece. If asked, students will admit that they usually write their outlines after finishing the drafts. There is nothing wrong with this. Outlines are excellent revision tools. The problem with outlines is that they don't help the novice get started writing. And starting a piece of writing feels like pinning clouds to a bulletin board. It's hard to know what to tack down first. Every student asks the same questions: How can I research before I know what I am going to say? How do I know what to say until I outline? How can I outline until I know what I am going to say?

It's difficult to advise students how to proceed. Nowhere are experienced writers less consistent than in preparing to write. They talk about it; they refuse to talk about it. They make outlines; they hate them. They write 70,000-word summaries; they try to find just one word. They barely research; they collect volumes. They start drafting from the beginning and write to the end; they won't start drafting until they finish the last page. They plan little by little between drafting sessions; they plan everything before they begin. They call what they do before they write by a thousand different names: *planning, outlining, research, narrowing the topic, finding a slant, preliminary drafts, prewriting,* or *incubating.* Every writer and every piece is different—not a reassuring or helpful thought for a beginner wondering what to do next with a handful of clouds.

Teachers often try to help students with story-starters or narrowly defined topics. This doesn't work. Only a few students in any group are inspired by the story-starter or the topic. None of them learn to do their own thinking. In the long run, it is easier to lead students step-by-step through each point of the writing idea triangle in chapter 1 at least once. After all, what all writers really want from planning is a crystal clear writing idea. Once you gently lead students all the way through the planning process, you can joyfully toss the story-starters and topics out the window.

The Writing Idea Triangle Revisited

Each piece of writing is a new adventure. No one can anticipate everything with planning. Students, who have not had much writing experience, are even less likely to know what to plan for.

25

The three points of the triangle give them an easy way to organize the planning steps. Covering all three points, at least lightly, ensures that they cover the ground that might appear once they start writing. (We fudged in chapter 1 on the names of the points of the triangle; they really are *focus*, *background*, and *order*, as shown in illustration below.)

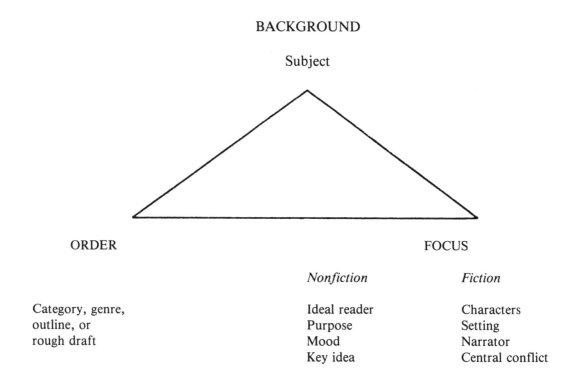

BACKGROUND

Subject

ORDER

FOCUS

	Nonfiction	*Fiction*
Category, genre,	Ideal reader	Characters
outline, or	Purpose	Setting
rough draft	Mood	Narrator
	Key idea	Central conflict

Choosing important elements of the writing helps students find a *focus*, so that they know what their piece is about. Researching the subject gives students the *background* material and vocabulary needed to write fluently. Because writing is sequential, the *order* point of the triangle includes anything that gives the writer clues as to what will come first and what will come next. It can be as vague as a genre or as specific as a first, rough draft. Outlines fall somewhere in between.

In theory, thoroughly tacking down each point of the writing idea triangle would clarify the idea to the point where drafting the piece would be secondary, and no revision would be necessary. In practice, the plan may never be finished until the third or fourth revision.

The background of a piece is large and vague. Without some guides, students flop around in pools of information never quite knowing what to do with it all. The prewriting choices, on the other hand, are specific and easy to make. Choosing them early narrows the field of research considerably, so we usually start at the *focus* point of the triangle, then move to researching in the *background*. We always tackle the *order* corner of the triangle last—if at all. It is the most difficult corner for students and writers alike. Many people must start writing and organize while they edit. In theory, one could start at any point of the triangle; in practice, *focus, background*, then *order* usually works best.

This chapter has three main sections, based on the writing idea triangle: "Finding a Focus," "Background Research," and "Finding an Order." Each contains a potpourri of useful prewriting activities and handouts from which to choose. The only two activities we consider absolute necessities are the first two because they introduce students to the prewriting choices.

Before you start, take a tip from us. Leading students through the planning process the first time is much easier if you start with very short pieces on ideas of *their own choosing*. Make sure students writing nonfiction choose a simple subject with which they are familiar. If possible, steer them toward genres with a strong sense of order, such as a "how-to," "ten tips on ... ," "question/answer," etc. Avoid biographies, reports, essays, and other complex genres. Steer students writing fiction toward stories with one or two main characters in a familiar setting.

FINDING A FOCUS

The prewriting choices have two things in common: they are crucial decisions all writers must make, and accidentally changing even one of them in the middle of the draft will *always* result in a major rewrite or a confusing disaster. Writing involves many decisions, but these particular choices operate a bit like the artist's horizon line and perspective points. They aren't terribly difficult choices to make, but making them aligns the perspective of the rest of the work. They make writing so much easier for students that we consider them the most important contribution we make to a student's writing. The prewriting choices are:

Nonfiction	*Fiction*
Ideal reader	Characters
Purpose	Setting
Mood	Narrator
Key idea	Central conflict

Activity 1:
Prewriting Choices for Nonfiction

i never think at all when i write / nobody can do two things at the same time / and do them both well.

—Don Marquis

There is an old saying among writers: "Nonfiction starts hard and ends easy; fiction starts easy and ends hard." It's true for students too. They have a terrible time starting nonfiction and an equally bad time finishing fiction. Teachers first give students longer nonfiction assignments in middle school, and it's a hard start. More often than not, the results look like scrambled eggs with minced encyclopedia.

Stories can grow from what happens first and what happens next. That rarely happens in nonfiction. Getting a clear focus is 90 percent of the nonfiction battle. Once students get off to a little easier start, many of them prefer writing nonfiction, and their work always improves. Here we present a nonfiction choices checklist and a handout to help them.

These handouts are long. If your budget is short for such things, you can use the prewriting checklist and give a verbal explanation. We like to send the full-length handouts home with students because few stories are finished without a little help from Mom and Dad. Parents are often grateful for clues on how to help their children without writing the piece for them.

Instructions to Students

When you write, you make many decisions. You make little decisions, such as what word to use in a sentence, and big decisions, such as choosing a writing idea. There are certain other decisions you should make before you go very far. We call these *the prewriting choices* because you should always make them *before* you start to write. For nonfiction, you choose your ideal reader, purpose, mood, and key idea. You don't know it now, but you'll see later that making these decisions early makes writing nonfiction much easier.

Sit with your writing group today (see "Teacher's Notebook: On Writing Groups and Writing Conferences," p. 37). We're going to go through each choice and explain it. Then you need to make the choice for your own piece. You each have a "Prewriting Checklist." As you make your decisions, record them on the checklist and discuss them with your writing group. Be sure to write in pencil, so that you can change your mind.

NONFICTION PREWRITING CHOICES CHECKLIST

My writing idea is: _____

_____ .

1. **IDEAL READER**
   My ideal reader is: _____ .
   I chose this ideal reader because: _____

   _____

   _____ .

2. **PURPOSE**
   The purpose of this piece is to: _____

   _____

   _____

   _____ .

   My ideal reader would like to read this because: _____

   _____

   _____ .

3. **MOOD**
   The mood of this piece is: _____

   _____ .

4. **KEY IDEA**
   My key idea is: _____

   _____

   _____ .

NONFICTION PREWRITING CHOICES (HANDOUT)

1. IDEAL READER. Who is going to read your piece? Thinking of one particular person as you write helps you decide what to say. Suppose your writing idea is "how to make a peanut butter and jelly sandwich." You would say one thing to a five-year-old, who has never made one, and something completely different to a cafeteria worker, who has made hundreds.

   When you choose an ideal reader, you can choose a real person or make up an imaginary one. It is usually easier to choose someone who knows less about your subject than you; for example, someone younger than you, someone who is learning about your subject for the first time, or one of your fellow students who hasn't read about it yet. *Don't choose your teacher.* You will keep wondering what to say that the teacher doesn't already know. When you choose your ideal reader, ask yourself, "Why do I know more about this than my ideal reader?" It helps.

2. PURPOSE. Why are you writing this piece? Why would your ideal reader want to read it? Do you want to entertain your reader? to show your reader how to do something? to persuade your reader to do something? to describe something your reader hasn't seen? Answer these questions, and you will know your purpose.

   Think of your writing as a gift. You give your gift to your ideal reader. *Your purpose is what you plan to give.*

   EXAMPLES

   - to *entertain* my ideal reader
   - to *show* my ideal reader *how something works*
   - to *show* my ideal reader *how to* do something
   - to *persuade* my ideal reader to do something
   - to *report* what happened to my ideal reader
   - to *give my opinion* on something to my ideal reader
   - to *explain* to my ideal reader *why* I have that opinion
   - to *describe* something to my ideal reader
   - to *trace the history* of something for my ideal reader
   - to *show* my ideal reader *why (or how) two things are the same*
   - to *show* my ideal reader *why (or how) two things are different*

   You can also have two purposes, for example, "to explain how to do something in an entertaining way," "to give my opinion and explain why," or "to describe something and trace its history."

3. MOOD. A piece of writing is like a good conversation. It shares a mood as well as ideas. You can be friendly and helpful. You can go on a crusade for your ideas. You can be detached and logical. You can be funny and informal. Think of sitting down with your ideal reader over lunch and talking with him or her about your writing idea. What kind of mood do you want your conversation to have?

EXAMPLES

humorous	informative	silly
crusading	ironic	angry
friendly	· helpful	detached
leisurely	quick	commanding
critical	serious	sad

4. KEY IDEA. Your *key idea* is your writing idea. Any article, essay, or book should be about just one key idea. Everything else in the piece is tied to that idea. To choose your key idea, you can either copy down your original writing idea or use the decisions you've made about the ideal reader, purpose, and mood to sharpen it up. The sharper your idea, the easier it is to write nonfiction.

EXAMPLES

Original Writing Idea:　How to make a peanut butter and jelly sandwich.

Key Ideas:　　　　　　How to make forty peanut butter and jelly sandwiches in no time flat.

How to make your first peanut butter and jelly sandwich.

How to make low-calorie peanut butter and jelly sandwiches.

A day in the life of a peanut butter and jelly sandwich.

Original Writing Idea:　What freedom means to me.

Key Ideas:　　　　　　Freedom gives people rights *and* responsibilities.

Freedom must be practiced every day.

Freedom is enjoying the little things in life.

Freedom is having dreams of your own.

A story of one person's escape to freedom.

Original Writing Idea:　Getting good grades.

Key Ideas:　　　　　　Why students should try to get good grades.

A survey asking teachers why they give grades.

Ten tips for getting better grades.

What to do when you get a bad grade.

A story of a person's first *A*.

Sharpening up your key idea takes a little practice. Sometimes it helps to pretend that you are holding a camera. Suppose your subject is trees. Are you going to talk about the big wide-angle picture, panning back to show the whole forest and perhaps, trace its history? Or are you going to use a narrow lens and focus on the story of just one tree in that forest? Perhaps you'll tell the story of something in between — of one type of tree in that forest or of all the trees along one stream.

Think, too, about the period of time involved. If you are going to discuss one tree, are you going to cover its whole history going back to the Ice Age? Or are you going to show what happens in and around that tree during spring, summer, fall, and winter? What about just one day in the life of that tree?

It sometimes helps to try to think of several key ideas that might work, then choose the best one. Remember to *choose just one key idea.* You can only tell one story at a time. Two will be confusing and very hard to write.

Activity 2:
Prewriting Choices for Fiction

Why shouldn't *truth be stranger than fiction? Fiction, after all, has to make sense.*

—Mark Twain

To anyone who loves writing, teaching twelve- to fifteen-year-olds to write fiction is a great joy. They never run out of ideas; their enthusiasm is infectious; and their capacity for absorbing some of the technical aspects of writing fiction is astonishing. Seventh and eighth graders may be a little shaky on nonfiction, but fiction is ice cream and candy to most of them.

Better yet, writing fiction puts pressure on their vocabularies and encourages them to use more complex sentences. The logical demands of fiction stress connecting cause and effect. Students may learn more about science from science fiction and more about history from historical fiction than they will from reports or papers. Fiction is an ideal vehicle for teaching middle school and early high school skills and concepts. Teachers don't use it enough.

Students this age have no trouble thinking up plots. They'll stuff every story with four or five plots. "But I may never get to write another story," one complained when we pointed out that he had enough characters and plots for ten stories. It's really impossible to plan stories too far ahead, so the principal purpose for the fiction prewriting choices is to help students sort out just one story to tell.

Instructions to Students

Sit with your writing groups. Today we're going to learn to make the prewriting choices for fiction: characters, central conflict, setting, and narrator. We're going to go through each choice and explain it, then you need to make the choice for your own story. You each have a prewriting checklist. As you make your decisions, record them on the checklist and discuss them with your group. Be sure to write in pencil, so that you can change your mind.

(Text continues on page 36.)

FICTION PREWRITING CHOICES CHECKLIST

My writing idea is: _____

_____ .

1. CHARACTERS
   The name of my main character is (first, middle, and last): _____

   _____ .

   My main character wants: _____

   _____ .

   The names of my secondary characters are:

   _____

   _____

   _____

2. CENTRAL CONFLICT
   The central conflict of my story is: _____

   _____ .

   The story ends when: _____

   _____ .

   The crisis comes when:_____

   _____ .

   The story begins when:_____

   _____ .

3. SETTING(S)
   My story is set in (name the big setting or settings): _____

   _____

   _____

   _____ .

   List possible little settings within the big setting(s): _____

   _____

   _____

   _____

   _____

   _____ .

   The setting is _____important _____not important.

4. NARRATOR
   My narrator (first person) is the character in my story named: _____ .
   My narrator (third person) is a person outside the story who is retelling it_____ .

STORY STATEMENT—This is a story about: _____

_____

_____ .

FICTION PREWRITING CHOICES (HANDOUT)

1. **CHARACTERS**

Stories are about imaginary people. Even if your story is about animals or creatures from another planet, the animals or creatures act like people. The imaginary people, animals, or creatures in your story are called *characters*. The most important characters in your story are your main character and your secondary characters.

The Main Character

The most important character in your story is called the *main character.* You can only have *one* main character. The main character has a problem to solve, wants something, or tries to do something. This is called the central conflict. In the *Wizard of Oz*, for example, Dorothy wants to get home to Kansas. In *E.T.*, E.T. wants to phone home. In the Sherlock Holmes stories, Holmes wants to solve the mystery. Your first prewriting decision is to choose your main character. What does your main character want? That's your central conflict.

The Secondary Characters

The *secondary characters* are the other important characters besides the main character. For example, the Tin Man, the Scarecrow, and the Lion are secondary characters in the *Wizard of Oz*. Elliot, the little boy who helps *E.T.*, and Dr. Watson in the Sherlock Holmes stories are also secondary characters. You can choose just one or two secondary characters or a whole crowd of them.

The difference between the secondary characters and the main character is that the central conflict belongs to the main character. The Tin Man and Scarecrow help Dorothy get to Kansas. They just happen to solve some of their own problems along the way.

You don't need to have a secondary character, but, if you choose more than one or two, be careful not to have too many. One or two is usually more than enough to make a good story.

Minor Characters and Bit Players

There are two other types of characters that you should know about, although you don't need to make any decisions about them right away. You can make them up as you write. These are *minor characters* and *bit players*.

Minor characters usually have names. The reader learns a little bit about them, but not much. For example, the Wizard and all the witches in the *Wizard of Oz* are minor characters. Villains are often minor characters. In *E.T.*, Elliot's mother is a minor character. Sherlock's clients are minor characters.

Bit players, on the other hand, are hardly people at all. They do their little bit for the story and disappear. They open the gates to Oz, drive taxis to the airports, answer questions at hotel desks. They usually don't even have names.

You can think of your main and secondary characters as round characters. The reader knows all about them in detail. They are rounded out. The minor characters and bit characters are flat. Your reader never learns very much about them; they are just there to move the story forward in some way.

(Handout continues on page 34.)

2.   THE CENTRAL CONFLICT

The central conflict is your main character's biggest problem. It's easiest to think of a central conflict by asking yourself, "What does my main character want? Does he or she want to do something? to solve a problem? to get something? to make something?" That's your central conflict. When your main character gets what he or she wants, your story ends. (Sometimes your main character doesn't get what he or she wants. The story ends once it's clear that the main character will never get it.)

Beginners often make the mistake of creating several central conflicts. Stick to just one. Just because you choose one central conflict doesn't mean there won't be plenty of other problems for your characters to solve. Dorothy didn't make it home to Kansas without bumping up against witches and dark forests. Secondary characters have their problems, too. The Tin Man wanted a heart, and the Scarecrow wanted a brain. But the central conflict, the problem that started everything else, was Dorothy's desire to go home.

Think of your story as a series of stair steps building up to a high point. Each step forward is another step to solving the main problem, but each step also has complications or setbacks to overcome. The story builds up to a final, big setback—a crisis. All seems lost. Then the main character overcomes the last setback, the central conflict is resolved, and the story quickly ends.

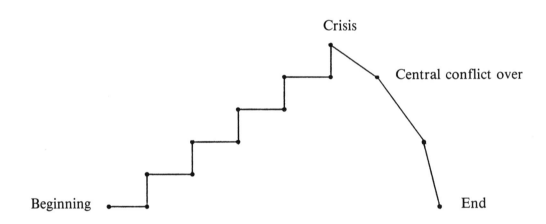

Because you know that the story ends once the central conflict is resolved, it may help you to decide how the story will end first. Then decide what the crisis point will be, and last of all, decide how to begin.

3.   SETTING

Your characters are *who* your story is about. The central conflict is *what* it is about. The setting is *where* it takes place.

Your story may have one setting or several. If you have more than one, it helps to think of settings as big settings and little ones. The big setting might be a town. The little ones might be the school, the local hardware store, or the town square. Your big setting might be a country. The little settings might be a city in that country, a small town in the mountains, or a roadside cafe on a main highway. If you are writing a science fiction story, your big setting might be another planet. The little settings might be various places on your planet.

You can have more than one big setting, but try not to use more than two or three. Once you choose a big setting, think of a list of two or three smaller settings within the big setting.

How important is setting to your story? If your story is set in an unfamiliar place, such as another planet or a far-off country, your setting might be very important. If your setting is uninteresting, such as a house that could be anywhere, the setting may not be very important. You decide.

4. NARRATOR

You have one more imaginary person to create before starting your story—the narrator. The narrator is the person who tells the story. Of course, in real life, you tell the story because you made it up, but readers like to pretend that stories really happened. They want to know why the person telling the story knows it. Is the narrator a character in the story and knows about it because he or she was there? Or is the narrator someone who found out about it and is retelling it?

If you pretend to be a character telling the story, your narrator will use *I* to tell the story. This is called a *first-person narrator*. If you pretend to be someone who found out about the story but wasn't part of it, your narrator will tell the story using *he* or *she*, not *I*. This is called a *third-person narrator*. (The third person narrator is sometimes called the "omniscient narrator." Omniscient means *all-knowing*. The omniscient narrator knows what every character did and thought.) The next time you read a story, notice the narrator. Is it a first-person narrator or a third-person narrator?

EXAMPLE

- "*I* walked the dog and then went to the store." (a first-person narrator: a character in the story named Mary)

- "*Mary* walked the dog, and then went to the store." (a third-person narrator)

Here are two pieces of good advice:

1. Create whichever narrator you like, but stick with the same narrator all the way through the story.

2. Pretend that your narrator is telling the story after the story is over (past tense). Don't pretend that your narrator is telling the story as it happens (present tense). It's hard to tell stories in the present tense.

EXAMPLE

- "I *walked* the dog, and then *went* to the store." (past tense)

- "I *walk* the dog, and then *go* to the store." (present tense)

Notes from the Pros:
On Writing to Length

Writing to length is one of the most difficult aspects of writing. The natural length of a story or of a nonfiction piece is a product of the prewriting choices. A change of one prewriting choice will change the length. An article on how to clean a carburetor aimed at mechanics is likely to be much shorter than the same article aimed at people who don't know what a carburetor is. With so many variables, it takes writers years—and plenty of editing—to be able to write a piece to an approximate length. Even then, they often make mistakes and must rewrite the entire piece. The shorter the piece, the harder it is to write to a specified length.

For these reasons, writers always advise teachers to avoid assigning lengths. It's work for experts. Instead of adjusting the prewriting choices, beginners will distort their writing by padding or inappropriate cutting if asked to produce a certain length. Teachers often don't listen to this advice, not because they especially love three-page or five-page papers, but because anxious students put tremendous pressure on them. "How long?" is the first question students ask about a writing assignment. They won't accept "as long as it takes" for an answer.

The writers are correct. Never assign lengths. You can try procrastination. Wait until students have finished planning or, even better, wait until they have produced a rough draft before caving into questions about length. If that wears thin, avoid assigning "pages." Instead, try using the categories of length used in the publishing industry:

FICTION LENGTH CATEGORIES

Category	Definition	Approximate Length
scene	a segment of a story	500-2,000 words
chapter	a section of a novel	1,500-7,500 words
vignette	a very short, but complete story	500-2,000 words
short story	a complete story, generally told from one viewpoint	1,500-7,000 words
novelette	a short novel	7,000-50,000 words
novel	a complete story told in several chapters, often from multiple viewpoints	50,000-150,000 words

NONFICTION LENGTH CATEGORIES

Category	Definition	Approximate Length
section	a segment of a nonfiction piece	100-1,500 words
chapter	a segment of a nonfiction book	1,500-7,000 words

Category	Definition	Approximate Length
filler (sometimes called a *short essay*, *short article*, or *anecdote*)	a very short, but complete piece	100-1,500 words
article (also called *a short piece* or *short essay*)	a complete piece of nonfiction on one aspect of a theme or topic	1,500-7,500 words
book	a complete piece covering several aspects of a theme	30,000-120,000 words
reference	a collection of information on a particular subject organized according to a pattern	no limits

In the world of the working writer, lengths are subject to publishing fads. The short story was king at the turn of the century, and 7,000 words was the most popular length. By World War II, the average length of the short story dropped to 3,000 words. Many short story writers found themselves unable to write to that length. Some abandoned the short story and turned to novels; others abandoned their careers.

The lengths in the chart are those used by professionals; for students, cut them to half or a third, depending on the age and writing experience of your students. Once students are used to the terms, they stop asking much about length.

Teacher's Notebook: On Writing Groups and Writing Conferences

Writing is a solo occupation, but writers still need friends with whom to share the process. Traditionally, they form writing groups to meet regularly and share work-in-progress. Students, too, can benefit from a writing group. At the beginning of the school year or term, break students into writing groups of no more than three to four students. Keep students together in their writing groups for the entire term.

The writing group should be responsible for helping each student in the group. Members of the group should be encouraged to serve as a sounding board for ideas, as assistants when the going gets rough, and as editors. Before students bring problems to the teacher, they should check with their writing group first. If the group cannot solve the problem, students should then make an appointment with the teacher.

Students do find talking over problems with the teacher reassuring. Try setting up a formal conference system as Donald Graves suggests in *Writing: Teachers and Children at Work*. Individual students or the entire writing group can make an appointment for a writing conference with the teacher during drafting or editing sessions. The appointment is important. It assures students that they will get a turn and also delays the conference just a little, so they may solve the problem on their own while they wait.

Graves also suggests that teachers conduct conferences with predictable steps:

1. Ask, "How can I help you?"

2. Let students try to express what is bothering them.

3. Read sections of their work aloud.

4. Discuss possible options and leave the decision to the student.

5. Keep the conference short, no more than five minutes.

Teacher's Notebook: On Writing Terms

Knowing a little jargon gives students a big boost. When they learn terms such as *character*, *fiction*, and *ideal reader*, they not only learn what choices to make but also have some way to talk about their writing. Just knowing that there are such things as *genres*, *settings*, *dialogue*, *action*, and *examples* inspires writing. Understanding what a *scene* is or what a *section* is helps them organize their work.

Teaching writing necessarily involves teaching terminology, but there are some significant problems with teaching writing jargon. First of all, writing terms are vague and don't hold up to precise definition. Most represent a decision made by writers, for good or ill. A sentence is anything the writer starts with a capital letter and ends with a period. It's impossible to be more specific. Not all sentences have a subject and a verb or represent a unified thought. Even runon and incomplete sentences are still sentences.

Secondly, no two writers, teachers, or editors use the same terms. They might call the *ideal reader* the *audience*, *reader*, or *market*. They might call the *key idea*, the *slant*, *angle*, *purpose*, *topic*, *subject*, *narrowed topic or subject*, or *lead*.

Finally, fiction and nonfiction writers need to know different terms. Critics use overlapping terms with a different emphasis. Discussing grammar or punctuation requires a set of terms aimed at dissecting sentences, useful only in the final stages of polishing.

Some writing teachers don't formally teach terms. They bring them up naturally during editing sessions and class discussion. Students gradually learn some terms on their own. We prefer to hand our students a few vital terms on a platter, so that the group has some common base from which to start discussing writing. Then we let the terminology flow with the class.

By the end of a semester or so, we like our students to know *categories* and *genres*, the *prewriting choices*, *scenes* and *sections*, and at least some of the techniques in chapter 4, such as *action*, *dialogue*, *examples*, and *anecdotes*. We teach grammar and punctuation separate from writing.

To overcome the circular definition problem while still giving students the terms up front, we use the same steps to teach every important term:

1. Define the term *briefly* and read several examples aloud to the group.

2. Ask students to try it in their practice journal (three to five minutes—no more).

3. Ask volunteers to share practice pieces with the group.

4. Pass out some kind of follow-up literature. We like handouts for important terms or lists of suggestions because students can refer to them later. Summaries on the blackboard or an overhead projection are fine for terminology questions in class.

BACKGROUND RESEARCH

Youngsters are long on imagination but short on information and vocabulary. With students between twelve and fifteen, the process of research is almost as important as the product. It's more than collecting information. Young students feel a great deal more pressure when they write than do adults because the physical process of writing is so much harder for them. Research gives them a chance to talk through possible sentences without writing them down, a sort of rough draft without the draft. Talking about the background helps them build up the vocabulary they will need to write the story.

All background research should include reading and as much discussion as possible. In general, the more students talk when they plan (and the less they talk when they draft), the easier writing is. (See also "Notes from the Pros: On Talking about It," p. 84.)

The first two activities in this section help students decide what to research. The third helps them find readily available "experts" to interview. The fourth one helps fiction students round out their major characters, and the last three are bald-faced vocabulary builders.

Activity 3:
The Knowledge Chart

As is our confidence, so is our capacity.
—William Hazlitt

Breaking the subject down into bite-sized chunks is always the best first step to research. We use this very simple activity to help students chart out what they know and what they don't know about a subject or a writing idea, so they can think about the information they need to gather.

Instructions to Students

Now that you've made your prewriting choices, you have a focus and you know what you are going to write about. What are you going to say? Well, you might have some ideas, but you don't have all of them yet. Today, we're going to start researching the background for your stories and nonfiction pieces. Think of your key idea or your central conflict as the foreground. It's right up front. To fill in all the details, you need to study the background. Nonfiction writers research the subject; fiction writers research the setting or the details of the characters' lives. Research not only helps you think of things to say, it also gives you confidence. You know what you are talking about because you read about it and thought it through before you started writing.

Where do you start research? Make a list of the things you *already* know about the subject. What about the things you don't know? Make another list. Finally, make a list of things you need to find out. It's that simple. To make it even easier, we've passed out a knowledge chart so that you can record your lists in one place (see the illustration on p. 40).

Those of you writing nonfiction can make your lists about your subject: peanut butter sand-wiches, hot air balloons, turtles, and so forth. Fiction writers can use the setting, the history of the characters, or some event in the story.

EXAMPLE

NAME: *JB Student*

WRITING IDEA: *Raising Turtles as a Hobby*

DATE:

WHAT I KNOW	WHAT I DON'T KNOW	NEED TO FIND OUT
· Reptiles - Like water, mud - Have hard shells - Several types: snapper box green tortoise - They are an old species	-How they fit in the ecological chain - what they eat -How old they get - Which types make good pets	- ecological chain - foods for different types of turtles - oldest turtle - Why make good pets and why not - what makes a good pet - where buy best types

Activity 4:
Research Strategy

Time given to thought is the greatest time-saver of all.
—Norman Cousins

Research is an art of its own. Without help, few students get much beyond copying the encyclo-pedia at this age, yet they need the information research yields in order to write. What teachers need is a simple way to get students started. We use the research strategy. Like the knowledge chart, it breaks the research down, but it also introduces students to the idea of sources and encourages them to inter-view people, make their own observations, and use books other than the encyclopedia.

Instructions to Students

Research is a fancy-sounding word for collecting facts, ideas, and information. You can research by reading books, talking to people, or observing something yourself. The books, people, and observations are called *sources*.

You could just go to a library and read any book on your subject, but even the school media center is a big place. You can't read every book in it. You need to choose a few. Just talking to anybody won't do. You need to find an expert who knows what you want to know. What you need is a strategy to decide what to read and who to consult before you start.

There are three parts to a research strategy: *areas*, *pointers*, and *sources*. Areas are broad categories you want to study. Pointers are ideas about what to study within each category, and sources are the books you read or the people you ask (see the illustration below).

EXAMPLE

NAME: *JB Student*

WRITING IDEA: *What to do when you get a bad grade*

DATE:

AREAS	POINTERS	POSSIBLE SOURCES
What to do	*what do teachers say students should do?* *what do good students do?* *what do poor students do?*	*teachers* *good students* *poor students*
Bad grade	*what is a bad grade?* *Why do teachers give bad grades?*	*counselors* *teachers* *survey of student opinion*

HOW TO MAKE UP A RESEARCH STRATEGY

There are four steps to making up your research strategy:

1. Break your writing idea down into areas to study.

2. Make a list of pointers.

3. Write down possible sources.

4. Make a notebook and choose priorities.

STEP 1.   Break your story statement or key idea into areas to study.

Go back to your prewriting choices checklist and copy your story statement or your key idea statement on a separate sheet of paper. Next, underline all the important words and phrases in your story statement or key idea. Write those words down in a list. If you are not sure if a word is important, underline it. You can always cross it off the list later.

EXAMPLE (Nonfiction)

Key Idea—"What to do when you get a bad grade."

    what to do

    bad grade

EXAMPLE (Fiction)

Story Statement—"This is a story about some people who crash their plane in the Amazon and fight their way through the jungle back to a small town."

    crash

    plane

    Amazon

    fight

    jungle

    small town

Now you have a list of the areas you want to study.

STEP 2:   Make a list of pointers. (*Note:* If this is too difficult, use the knowledge chart activity 3 first.)

Bad grade, crashes, and planes are big subjects. You won't need to know everything about them for your story. Pointers narrow the area down and point out the types of things within that area you might want to learn. Write a few pointers for each area.

EXAMPLE (Nonfiction)

Areas	*Pointers*
what to do	What do teachers say students should do?
	What do good students do?
	What do poor students do?
bad grade	What is a bad grade?
	Why do teachers give bad grades?

EXAMPLE (Fiction)

Areas	*Pointers*
crash	What makes planes crash?
	What would the pilot do in a crash?
plane	What kind of plane would be a good one for the story?
	How many passengers do various small planes hold?
Amazon	What part of the Amazon has jungle near it and a good small town to head for?
	What sort of people live there? What language do they speak?
	What's the weather like?
fight	What sort of tools and supplies would be needed to survive, say, ten days in the jungle?
	What kind of food would the passengers be able to hunt or pick? How would they go about it?
jungle	What does it look like?
	What are the names of some of the plants?
	What are the dangers of the jungle?
small town	What does it look like?
	Would it have an airport? boats?
	Would the town people be different from the jungle people?

STEP 3.   Make a list of possible sources.

There are three types of sources:

1.   *Experts.* An expert doesn't need a Ph.D. An expert is just a person who knows about the area you are researching. For example, you could talk to a pilot about planes and airplane crashes. You might know someone who visited the Amazon on vacation.

2.   *Personal Observation.* You can make yourself into an expert by taking a look on your own and making notes. If you are going to write about peanut butter and jelly sandwiches, try making one for research. You could go to the Amazon if you could afford the trip, but you could also watch a television program about the Amazon and take notes. You can also look at planes in a local museum. Observation includes doing your own experiments and taking your own surveys.

3.   *Books, articles, and films.* Almost everything you need can be found in some library somewhere. The school media center is a small library. Your local public library is bigger. There are also some huge libraries, such as the Library of Congress. Use your research strategy to show the media center specialist what information you need. The media specialist can help you choose the proper books or films.

Look at each area on the list and think about the kind of questions you need to answer. Is there an expert nearby you could interview? Can you personally observe something or take your own survey? Write down the type of expert or personal observation idea next to each area. Write books, articles, or films next to the others.

EXAMPLE (Nonfiction)

Areas	*Possible Sources*
what to do	teachers
	good students
	poor students
bad grade	counselors (what is a bad grade)
	teachers (what is a bad grade)
	survey of student opinion

EXAMPLE (Fiction)

Areas	*Possible Sources*
crash	a pilot
plane	a book on airplanes
Amazon	a filmstrip about the Amazon

STEP 4.   Make a notebook and choose priorities.

Research takes time. You may run out of time to research, so you will want to cover the most important areas first and the least important areas last.

Make a little notebook with one page for each area. Write the area, your pointers, and your sources at the top of the page. You can use the bottom of the page for taking notes. Shuffle your pages so that your notebook has the most important area first, the next most important area second, and so forth.

Now you are set to go. Your notebook reminds you what to research, whom to ask, and which things to find out first. Be sure to write down which books you *actually* read and which experts you actually consult. Sources don't always work out as you plan. You'll need to adjust your sources depending on who or what you find later on.

Activity 5:
Finding Expert Sources

Everybody is ignorant, only on different subjects.
— Will Rogers

Everyone is an "expert" to a writer. It's just a matter of discovering the subject. Hang around writers on their daily rounds, and you'll find them asking the store clerk how the new shoes are working out, debating menu changes with the owner of the local cafe, and sympathizing with the bus driver over schedule changes. Bums will not get a quarter from a writer without first explaining where to sleep on the street. After all, writing after doing library research is not the same as writing after discussing the subject with an expert source.

The students, families, and teachers of the average class form a vast pool of experts. Between them, they have traveled to all corners of the globe, learned to speak several languages, built everything from log canoes to high rises, done every job from timberjack to politician. They know how to grade diamonds and make soda pop; they have lived through wars, fires, tornadoes, depressions, and floods.

For students, interviewing an expert source makes writing twice as much fun. We use this activity to create a class file of home-grown experts who are willing to be interviewed by students during the rest of the school year. Making the file gives students valuable experience with interviewing and a whole different view of the so-called "average" people around them.

Before you start, prepare copies of the "Class Experts Questionnaire" and the "Outside Experts Questionnaire" and warn your fellow teachers that they are about to be pestered by writing students with a bunch of personal questions. (For younger students, you may also want to type up an explanatory letter that they can take with them.) Be sure to pair students in interview teams. It's much easier for students to overcome sudden attacks of shyness, to remember what to ask, and to record the answers with two interviewers.

Choose some convenient method for filing and cross-referencing the written interviews by name and area of expertise.

Instructions to Students

Experts are all around you. Consulting one may not be as hard as you think. The "Expert Sources File" is a class project. What we need is a list of people who are willing to talk to students. We also need to find out each person's area of expertise. Once we have the file, members of the class can use it to locate expert sources when they write up research strategies.

Everyone you know is an expert on something. Did you know that one of the teachers in your school was a professional rodeo cowboy? Another one works on an archaeological dig in England every summer. Another collects precious stones. We know that one of your parents runs an ice cream factory, another is a secretary for a big corporation, and another works at city hall. These people are experts. Rodeos, archaeology, precious stones, ice cream, big corporations, and city hall are their areas of expertise. When you write stories, you might want to research any one of these areas by talking with an expert source.

How do you find out what a person's area of expertise is? You ask questions; for example, "What jobs have you held?" When the answer is "rodeo cowboy," you know that this person could be an expert for a student writing a story with a rodeo in it. One person might be an expert in several areas. That's what you are going to do for this project: ask people questions and figure out their areas of expertise.

To do this project, you will pair up with another student and interview at least two other people you know. Once you collect everyone's interviews, you will fill in the space at the top of the interview with a list of that person's areas of expertise.

In-class Experts

The first experts we know are—ourselves. How many of you have lived in another town? have gone to another school? have a hobby outside school? know about something that the rest of the class might not know about? Fill out the class experts questionnaire for our expert sources file.

Don't think that you need a Ph.D. in an important field to be an expert. Your fellow classmates may need to know about little things too. If you collect stamps or raise ants, put it down. Some mystery writer may need to know about stamps; some science fiction writers may need to know about ants.

We've left a big space at the bottom of the questionnaire. If you think of a good question to ask your fellow students, come up and write it on the blackboard. All of you can use the space at the bottom of your questionnaires to answer any of the questions on the board. (Note: We always get the board questions started by asking, "What's the hardest thing you've ever had to do?")

CLASS EXPERTS QUESTIONNAIRE

Fill in this section after you've finished answering the questions.

Areas of expertise: _____   _____

_____   _____

_____   _____

Name: (first and last) _____

When is the best time to talk to you? _____

List the number of your home room and the name of your home room teacher. _____

1. Have you ever lived in another town? where? How long ago did you live there? How old were you when you lived there?

2. Do you know any languages other than English?

3. Is any one in your family from another town? another country?

4. What's your favorite subject in school? Have you ever done anything outside school related to your favorite subject?

5. Name three of your hobbies outside school.

6. What are the most interesting places you've been on vacation?

7. Do you belong to any organizations outside school, such as the Scouts, a karate club, a ham radio club, young astronauts, a band, etc.? List them.

8. Have you ever written enough about an area that you feel you could help others in the class who don't know about it?

9. If you were another student in the class trying to find an expert, what areas would you ask yourself about?

USE THE SPACE BELOW FOR ANSWERING QUESTIONS ON THE BOARD:

Outside Experts

You don't need to go very far to find outside experts. Besides your fellow students, you can also use teachers, parents, and neighbors as experts. Don't forget grandparents, aunts, and uncles who live nearby. When you first talk to an outside expert, *be sure* to explain what you are doing. First, ask if the person would be willing to be interviewed by students who are researching stories. If the answer is "no," say "thank you" and choose another person. Once your expert source says "yes," then explain that you are trying to find out the areas in which he or she might have some special expertise.

OUTSIDE EXPERTS QUESTIONNAIRE

(Note to interviewers: Fill in this section after you've finished the interview.)

Areas of expertise: _____   _____

_____   _____

_____   _____

1. What is your name?

2. When and where could a student contact you?

3. If students writing stories or magazine articles need to talk with an "expert," what subjects do you think you could help them with?

4. What is your job?

5. Have you held other jobs that students might want to ask you about?

6. Do you have any special hobbies?

7. Have you ever built anything?

8. Have you ever learned to fix anything; for example, cars or household appliances?

9. Have you ever lived anyplace besides here? where?

Interviewed by: _____

(Note to interviewers: Be sure to say "Thank you.")

Activity 6:
Giving Your Characters a Background

*The characters have their own lives and their own logic and
you have to act accordingly.*

— Isaac Bashevis Singer

Students often assume that the name makes the character. Even their main characters are completely flat. This little activity helps fiction students get to know some of the things that go into rounding out a character. Students enjoy it for obvious reasons and often want to keep writing, so leave plenty of extra time.

Instructions to Students

Whatever happens in your story happens because of a character. Your characters act or react to something. They take those actions because of their background: their previous experiences, their opinions, and their personalities. Characters are just like real people. They have names, live somewhere, hold jobs, go to school, own pets, and have pet peeves. They even get tired and cranky.

Part of the fiction writer's background research is getting to know the characters. It's easy to do. Just answer some questions about your characters.

The "Character Interview" handout has a list of questions to ask. The questions are written as questions *to* the characters. Pair up with another student in the class. To use the handout, one of you asks the questions while the other pretends to be a character from his or her story answering the questions. Don't forget to write down the answers. When you have finished a character, exchange places.

INTERVIEW WITH A CHARACTER (HANDOUT)

1. Are you the main character in the story or a secondary character?

2. What is your full name (*first*, *middle*, and *last*)?

3. Do you have a nickname? What is it? How did you get that nickname?

4. How does your name fit your personality? Do you like your name? Even your middle name?

5. How old are you? What year were you born?

6. Where do you live? Do you live alone or with other people? Who lives with you? Are the people you live with characters in the story?

7. Do you have a job? What is it? Where do you work? What are the hours? How long have you done that job? What did you do before? Do you like your job?

8. Do you go to school? What grade? What's your best subject? What's your worst? Do you like school?

9. How tall are you? What build (thin, medium, heavy, etc.)? How much do you weigh? What color is your hair? Your eyes?

10. Are you rich, poor, or average? Does it matter to you whether or not you have money?

11. Which three of the following traits best describe you:

lazy	clumsy	cheerful	tense	shy
loyal	imaginative	snobbish	good-natured	generous
intelligent	curious	enthusiastic	neat	angry
graceful	unhappy	powerful	careful	thoughtful
lonely	tight-fisted	detached	dull	tough
practical	messy	timid	bold	frustrated
funny	relaxed	critical	sympathetic	outgoing
bubbly	loud	quiet	hard-working	artistic
organized	energetic	intellectual	confused	
realistic	a dreamer	fussy	serious	

12. What would you like most if you could have it?

13. What is your biggest pet peeve?

14. What do other people always tell you about yourself?

15. What is the best thing about you? The worst?

16. When are you happiest?

17. Choose any three of your answers and write two or three paragraphs explaining those answers.

Activity 7:
Making a Pictionary

Thought itself needs words.
It runs on them like beads on a string.
—Ugo Betti

The old tradition of handing out a list of vocabulary words for students to use in their stories doesn't work when every student is writing a different piece. It's just as well. The vocabulary never helped much anyway. It's hard enough for students to think of a good story without using certain words to tell it.

Making a pictionary is fun, but more important, it helps students collect vocabulary related to their pieces. It's easy to do—draw a picture of the subject, setting, characters, or anything else related to the piece and label all the components of the picture with words. Students can use a professional pictionary, such as *What's What* to look up more words for their pictures. For the unartistic, stick pictures on notebook paper work as well as fancy drawings. For the artistic, this activity may peak a little more interest in writing.

Instructions to Students

What's a pictionary? It's a dictionary of pictures with all the words written in. Making a pictionary helps you write because you learn words you need for your story before you start. Making a pictionary is simple. Draw a picture of something in your story. You could draw a picture of the subject, your characters, or the setting. Then label everything in the picture with words. Make a list of all the words in the picture (see the two illustrations below).

There is a book on the reference shelf called *What's What*. It's a pictionary on all sorts of subjects. You can look in it for more words you might need for your story and add them to your list. If you don't know how to spell a word, look up the correct spelling before you write it in your pictionary. You all know how to use *The Misspeller's Dictionary* (Simon and Schuster, 1983). This is a good place to use it.

EXAMPLE

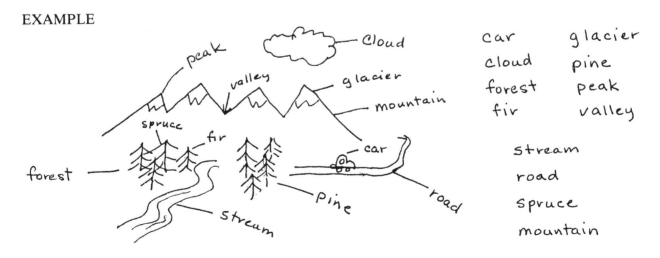

EXAMPLE

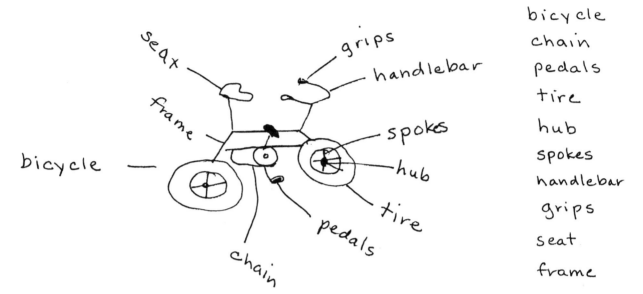

Activity 8:
Making a Verbiary

Words should be an intense pleasure,
just as leather should be to a shoemaker.
—Evelyn Waugh

The rule of style is: "Never use an adverb when a good strong verb will do." Verbs are the heart of the English sentence. The language makes up for its weak conjugation by allowing flexible use of its big vocabulary of verbs. A good vocabulary of verbs is the most important vocabulary for students to develop.

Making a verbiary builds a list of verbs students can use, but, more important, it imitates what they must do to think of verbs when they are writing. Although it's good practice, it is not an easy exercise. Show students how to do it before they start and plan on circulating from table to table filling in missing vocabulary with your own larger one.

Instructions to Students

In case you've forgotten, nouns are the words for people, places, and things. Verbs are the action of a sentence. They are what those people, places, and things do—even if they just sit there. In the sentence, "The dog jumped over the house," *dog* is a noun, *jumped* is a verb.

Look at the list of words from your pictionary. Most of them are nouns, aren't they? Today we're going to make a *verbiary* to go with your pictionary, just to make sure you've got plenty of verbs on hand for your story.

Sit with your writing groups today. We'll show you how to do this once before you try it on your own. Here is a handout to remind you of the steps.

MAKING A VERBIARY (HANDOUT)

STEP 1.   Find some verbs.

Write a list of just the nouns in your pictionary down the left-hand side of a piece of paper. Next to each one, write a simple sentence using that noun. Draw a line under the verb in your sentences.

EXAMPLE

peak — The man climbed the peak.

mountain — The mountain turned purple.

cloud — The cloud rained.

forest — The forest swayed in the wind.

road — The family drove up the road.

car — The car broke down.

stream — The stream flowed down the mountain.

STEP 2.   Turn the sentence around to make a silly sentence.

EXAMPLE

The peak climbed the man.

The rain clouded.

The wind swayed in the forest.

The road drove up the family.

Down broke the car.

The mountain flowed down the stream.

STEP 3.   Find a verb that *would* make sense.

Cross out the verb in each sentence. Then try to think of a verb that would make sense. Use your imagination. Fill in the new verb or rewrite the sentence to make sense. Underline the new verb.

EXAMPLE

The peak stopped the man.

The rain fell down.

The wind blew in the forest.

The road helped the family.

Down crashed the car.

The mountain spit out the stream.

(Handout continues on page 54.)

STEP 4.   Make a list of verbs.

You now have two lists of sentences with the verbs underlined. On a separate sheet of paper write down just the list of verbs. Next to each verb, write down any one of the following adverbs: quickly, slowly, angrily, suddenly, happily, sadly.

EXAMPLE

climbed quickly

turned angrily

rained happily

swayed quickly

drove angrily

broke sadly

flowed sadly

STEP 5.   Brainstorm to find new verbs.

Get together with your group. For each word, try to think up another way of saying it without the adverbs. List all the new verbs your group thinks up.

EXAMPLE

climbed quickly	ran
	dashed
	floated up
	danced
turned angrily	glared
	scowled
	frowned

Activity 9:
Making a Word-finder

[Words] can change their meanings right in front of you.
They pick up flavors and odors like butter in a refrigerator.
— John Steinbeck

Students are fascinated with synonyms. Few things increase their vocabulary faster than browsing through a thesaurus finding synonyms and antonyms for words they already know. Making a word-finder around words likely to come up in their writing not only provides them with a ready reference they understand (because they made it themselves), it also gives them a sense of power over the words in their story.

You'll need ten or fifteen copies of student dictionaries and about the same number of paperback thesauri. It's expensive, but if you can get several copies of Rodale's *Synonym Finder*, do so. We prefer the *Synonym Finder* to a thesaurus because it has so many more synonyms, and unlike the thesaurus, it arranges synonyms by definition.

Ask students to bring a pencil, their pictionary and verbiary lists (or any other vocabulary list), and a pack of 3-by-5-inch index cards. We normally avoid index cards, but it really is easier to make word-finders using them.

Students need help getting started reading the reference works. Be sure to model the activity once in front of the class, then pass out a handout of instructions to remind them of the steps (or write them on an overhead or the board). Plan on wandering around the classroom to help out. This activity takes time, but in terms of vocabulary learned, it's a real time-saver.

Instructions to Students

There are about 600,000 words in the English language, and we want you to learn them all by Friday. Just kidding. We do want to talk to you about words. The English language has more words than any other language in the world. This makes it a wonderful language for writing; there's always a perfect word sitting out there if you can find it. The more words you know, the easier it is to write. One of the things you should try to do before you start to write is to expand your vocabulary.

Your vocabulary is the number of words you know. You would be amazed how many words you already know—maybe 3,000 by the time you reach age twelve. You learn about a 1,000 words a year at your age without even trying, but you can speed up the process by making word-finders before you write. To make a word-finder, you start with the list of words you know from doing your pictionaries and verbiaries, then look in a synonym finder or a thesaurus and gather up more words to go with them.

The words you are going to gather are called *synonyms* and *antonyms*. A synonym is a word that means the same thing as another word. An antonym is a word that means the opposite. You may wonder why we have synonyms. Well, synonyms mean the same thing, but not exactly the same thing. For example, some synonyms for the word *blue* are turquoise, azure, navy, baby-blue, sapphire, and aquamarine. They are all blue, but they are different shades. Synonyms mean the same thing, but they have different shades of meaning.

There is another feature of words. The same word can mean two different things. Blue can mean the color blue or it can mean sad, as in "I'm feeling blue today." So the synonyms for blue can also be glum, unhappy, morose, dismal, bleak, or depressed.

Antonyms mean the opposite. There isn't any opposite for the color blue, but there is for the sad kind of blue: happy, delighted, cheerful, cheery, sunny, or positive.

Today we're going to make word-finders. This is your own list of synonyms and antonyms that you might want to use in your stories. Sit with your writing groups today. We've put a dictionary and a synonym finder or a thesaurus on each table. Get out your lists of pictionary and verbiary words and the 3-by-5-inch index cards we asked you to bring.

Always write word-finders in pencil, so you can erase. You can work alone or as a group taking turns. Here's a handout with the instructions and an example. When you finish today, put your cards in alphabetical order, put a rubber band around them, and store them in your folder so that you don't lose them.

MAKING A WORD-FINDER (HANDOUT)

<u>Reminders:</u>

- *Synonyms* are words that have nearly the same meaning but with slightly different shades of meaning.

- *Antonyms* are words that have the opposite meaning.

- A *dictionary* lists words alphabetically and explains what they mean. Words often have more than one meaning. Each new meaning of a word is numbered.
  BLUE
    1. a color
    2. sad or unhappy

- A *synonym finder* lists words alphabetically with synonyms for each word underneath. Each group of synonyms represents synonyms for a different meaning of the word.
  BLUE
    1. turquoise, azure, navy, baby-blue, sapphire, aquamarine
    2. glum, unhappy, morose, dismal, bleak, depressed

- A *thesaurus* is like a synonym finder, but it lists synonyms and antonyms, and it doesn't divide them up for different meanings like the synonym finder.
  BLUE
    syn.—turquoise, azure, navy, baby-blue, sapphire, aquamarine,
    glum, unhappy, morose, dismal, bleak, depressed
    ant.—happy, delighted, cheerful, cheery, sunny, positive

There are four steps to making a word-finder.

STEP 1.   Set up your index cards.

Choose a word from your pictionary or verbiary lists. Write it in big letters at the top of the index card. Make one card for each of the words from your pictionary and verbiary.

STEP 2.   Check the spelling and meaning in the dictionary.

Look up your first word in the dictionary. Check the spelling on your card. Correct it if you have it wrong. Read the definitions, so that you know what other meanings your word might have.

STEP 3 (for those using the thesaurus).   Find your synonyms and antonyms.

Look up your word in the thesaurus. Read the list of synonyms. These will be listed first next to the word "syn." Choose at least four synonyms that you like and write them on the index card. Don't just choose the first four. Choose short, punchy ones that *you like*.

Look for words listed next to "ant." These are the antonyms. Choose at least two or three that you like. Turn your index card over. Write "ant." at the top and write down your antonyms. Check the spelling.

EXAMPLE

(front of card)

syn.

PEAK

peak, summit, crest, ridge, mountaintop, cliff, tip, cap, spire

(back of card)

ant.

valley, depression, ravine, gully, river basin

STEP 3 (for those using the synonym finder).   Find your synonyms and antonyms.

Look up your word in the synonym finder. Read the list of synonyms. Choose four synonyms that you like and write them on the index card. Don't just choose the first four. Choose short, punchy ones that *you like*.

The synonym finder has only synonyms, so you must think up an antonym, then look up that word in the synonym finder. Choose two or three that you like. Turn your index card over. Write "ant." at the top and write down your antonyms. Check the spelling.

STEP 4.   Arrange cards alphabetically.

Arrange your word-finder cards in alphabetical order, then put a rubber band around them. Store them in your file folder.

Teacher's Notebook:
On Scenes and Sections

Outlines help everyone but the beginner. The major purpose of outlining is to break a piece of writing into smaller components (fiction *scenes* and nonfiction *sections*). Experienced writers can imagine what various scenes or sections might say as they outline. They can then use the outline to juggle the pieces into a sensible plan without a lot of rewriting. Beginners on the other hand have no idea what a scene or section might include until they write it. For them, outlining is like trying to put together a puzzle without any pieces. There are two completely separate writing skills involved: (1) writing solid fictional scenes or nonfiction sections in depth, and (2) fitting several scenes or sections together. To effectively outline, students need experience with both.

Young students don't have the patience to learn both skills in one assignment. Students writing complete pieces, however short, do not learn to write in depth. Instead of outlining, try jumping directly into isolated scenes and sections with your students (see chapter 4). Once students feel confident with scenes and sections, outlines make more sense. Teach students to write isolated scenes and sections and work back to complete pieces as they gain confidence and skill.

Teacher's Notebook: On Storing Papers

Lost papers cause hysteria in writing classrooms. Research notes and rough drafts soon create a blizzard of paper, much of it easily mistaken for scratch paper. The easiest way to solve the problem is to buy two cardboard banker's boxes: one for loose papers and one for portfolio pieces. Make two manila folders per student, one for each box.

Insist that students keep all their loose papers and their current practice journals in their folders. Keep the box of student folders out where they can retrieve whatever papers they need without asking. School lockers seem to eat stories for lunch, so it may be easiest to ask them to leave everything in the student box during the day and pick up anything they need for homework on the way home. A few will forget to come by after school, but that's a smaller crisis than a lost story.

Store clean, unmarked copies of portfolio pieces in the folders in the second box *under lock and key*. Keep them until the end of the year, then return the whole folder. Students are thrilled to see all the work they've done in a year. In the meantime, you'll have clean copies readily at hand for any publishing projects you have in mind (see "Teacher's Notebook: On Personal, Practice and Portfolio Journals," p. 10 and "Teacher's Notebook: On Simple Ways to Publish," p. 154).

FINDING AN ORDER

Writing is thinking on paper, but trying to draft and think simultaneously is difficult. Unlike thinking, writing is both linear and sequential; that is, it must be done one word at a time in a certain order. Thoughts, on the other hand, do not arrive one at a time in a particular sequence, but come at random, often arriving at inconvenient moments and disappearing when they are needed.

A prewriting outline is not really an attempt to organize the writing. That can only be done well during revision. When writers outline, they are attempting to remove the pressure to write and think simultaneously by handling some of the thinking ahead of time. They need to use outlining methods suited to that task.

To most teachers and their students, the word *outline* means the traditional topic outline:

   I.   First main topic

      A.   Subtopic

      B.   Subtopic

         1.   sub-subtopic

         2.   sub-subtopic

  II.   Second main topic

      A.   Subtopic

      B.   Subtopic

(Remember, you must have at least two subtopics.)

Though students should know what an outline is, as a tool to help people write, the topic outline is a nonstarter. It, too, is linear and sequential. In some ways, it is worse to use a topic outline than to write without an outline. Instead of helping the writer think through some of the relationships between ideas before writing about them, the topic outline attempts to classify and subordinate ideas. Ideas are not so docile: they declare independence in the middle of a draft. Minor point II.C.4. turns into a monster and chews up the First Main Topic while the Second Main Topic steadfastly insists on becoming a footnote. Then what?

If you want students to outline, try abandoning the topic outline and substituting a variety of outlining methods to help them collect their ideas before they start to write. Almost any method that serves one or more of the following purposes will do:

1. To collect facts and ideas in one place.

2. To break the piece into scenes or sections that can be written one at a time.

3. To organize ideas and information for easy retrieval.

Choosing a genre with a built-in sense of order is the simplest form of outlining. "How-to," "Ten tips on ... ," "A day in the life of ... ," and "questions and answers" all work well. Outlines do not need to be made before the draft; the first draft can serve as a useful outline. Outlining with a pair of scissors and a roll of tape is a time-honored tradition among writers. With word processors to take out some of the pain, cut and paste is gaining popularity. Branching, design, and the other alternatives covered in the following section are all simple ways to replace the topic outline without writing an entire draft.

Whatever method students choose, go easy on outlining. Many students do not have enough experience with writing to be able to anticipate it with an outline, and some people never can outline without first putting words on paper.

Activity 10:
Branching

One of the only virtues of linear outlining is that it looks neat, and that very virtue is its downfall. By working hard to make sure the outline is neat, we effectively cut off any additions and insertions, any new idea.

—Henriette Anne Klauser

Branching is one of the best outlining methods for quickly thinking ideas through and recording thoughts before they disappear. Its other virtue is that it produces a visible picture of a whole piece, so that students can begin to see where they are going.

This method is useful for brainstorming, outlining, or almost any other kind of planning. If you want more details on it, see Henriette Klauser's *Writing on Both Sides of the Brain* or Tony Buzan's *Use Both Sides of Your Brain*, which uses a similar method called *mind-mapping* primarily as a reading comprehension and study tool.

Instructions to Students

You can make writing easier if you take some time before you start to write to explore your ideas of what you might say. One easy way to do this is to make a branching outline (see the illustration below).

EXAMPLE

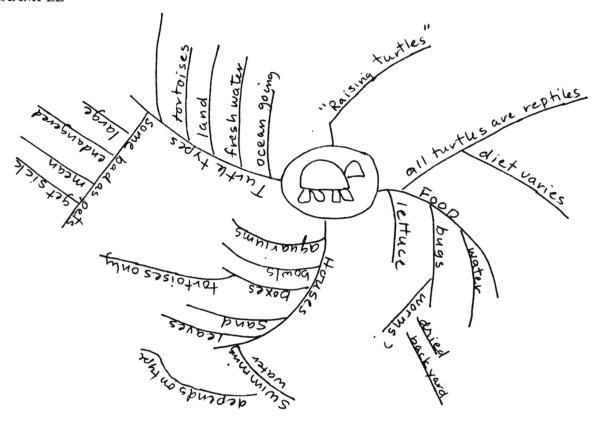

To make this branch, we started with our writing idea in the center and drew a picture of a turtle just for fun. We could have used the word turtle instead. The first thing we thought of was the title, "Raising Turtles." The next idea we had was that turtles need food, so we drew a branch for "Food" and collected our ideas about food on little branches shooting off the food branch. The idea of food suggested houses, so we made a branch for "Houses" and collected our ideas about turtle houses. We collected all of our ideas, no matter how trivial or silly they sounded. If we weren't sure about a fact, we just wrote a question mark after it.

We want you to try making a branch outline of your current story or nonfiction piece. There are not really any rules to follow, but here are some things to keep in mind:

- Begin in the center of the paper with a picture or a word representing your writing idea or some part of your writing idea.

- It is perfectly okay to be messy, to draw little pictures, to use colored pens, to use big pieces of paper, or anything else you wish. Don't try to be too pretty about it because that might slow you down. You want to collect your ideas as fast as you can. You can always draw a tidied-up branch later if you wish.

- Remember that ideas come in waves. If you run out of ideas, keep drawing branches and trying to fill them in until the next wave comes. Always try to branch for at least ten minutes, so that you catch more than one wave of ideas.

- You don't need to stick to one branch until you finish it. If an idea for another branch comes to mind, go to work on that branch for awhile.

- Record all your ideas, no matter how trivial or silly they seem at first. You can decide which ones to use later.

- Have fun. You'll be surprised by how much you know!

Activity 11:
The Design

To be simple is the best thing in the world;
to be modest is the next best thing.
I am not so sure about being quiet.
                  —G. K. Chesterton

Underlying most good nonfiction is a very simple design. Designs either break a nonfiction piece into manageable sections or suggest an order of presentation. Having some idea what those designs are helps many students begin to organize nonfiction.

You should not try to teach designs as an activity. Just pass out a handout and point out that students can use the notion of a design to help them outline. Designs will soon pop up in student work.

Instructions to Students

All nonfiction must have a simple plan, a logic behind the writing. This is not a complex outline, just a simple design. The writer makes up the design. It can be any design that the writer thinks will work. You can choose a design for your nonfiction piece, then use the design to help you write your outline. There are a thousand different designs. Here is a handout with some ideas of different types of designs you might want to use.

DESIGNS (HANDOUT)

Sequential design. This design is based on steps in the order (or sequence) of those steps. For example, a how-to article explains what to do first, second, and third in the order the reader is supposed to do them.

Past-present-future. This is a popular design where the writer reviews what happened in the past, what's happening now, and what is likely to happen in the future. Examples can be found in most science magazines, such as *Omni.* Lincoln's Gettysburg Address is another good example.

Most important point to least important point (or least important to most important). This plan is most often used to make a case for a key idea. For example, if you are writing a movie review, your key idea may be that the movie is bad. Using this design, you would either list first the most important reasons it is bad and work back to the least important. Or you can reverse the order, listing the least important reasons and working up to the most important.

Specific to general (or general to specific). This design starts with specific facts or examples and moves to more general statements (or vice versa). For example, if you are explaining how to fly a hot air balloon, you could tell the specific story of how one person does it and then show how this person's method follows general flying rules. You can also go the other way—explain the general rules for flying hot air balloons and give specific examples of one person doing it to illustrate those rules.

Three balanced points. This is the classic design of the traditional essay or paper. The writer chooses three to five points to make about the key idea and expands on each point equally, adding an introduction and a conclusion.

Storyplan. This design is written like a fictional story, but concludes by making a point. For example, you could tell a story about taking a hot air balloon flight, then discuss why people like the sport.

Musical design. This design is often used for speeches. Repetition of phrases or words carry the plan, so the speech sounds almost musical. One of the masters of this design was Martin Luther King, Jr. The best example is his "I Have a Dream" speech.

Activity 12:
Outlining Alternatives

He thinks things through very clearly
before going off half-cocked.
—General Carl Spatz

The number of outlining methods is limited only by the imagination.* We use this handout to encourage students to try some other methods of outlining besides branching and designs. Point out to students that different methods of outlining serve different purposes. They may want to make two or more outlines. The point is to come up with something that makes drafting the piece easier.

Instructions to Students

Writing a story or a nonfiction piece is an adventure, like going on a trip. Have you ever watched people plan for trips? They are very funny about it. Fenton Quagmire plans his trip by packing everything in the car he might possibly need, including a lot of junk he will never use. He buys maps of everything and tries to plan every step of the trip in little red lines. Betty Blastoff takes off with a dollar in her pocket and a box of cornflakes. She makes up the trip as she goes along.

Planning a piece of writing is just like planning for a trip. The outline is the place you store your maps and anything else you might need along the way.

Like Fenton, you can pack every little thing you might need into an outline, or you can blast off like Betty and make it up as you go along. Fenton and Betty are extremes. You may want to plan something in between. Do enough planning to decide the major points, but make up the details as you write. Here's a good rule of thumb to keep in mind: anytime you blast off without a plan, plan to do more editing than usual.

There are many different methods of outlining. We've already showed you branching and designs. Today we have a handout with some more outlining methods. You can use whichever method helps you the most. Remember, the only reason for making an outline is to make drafting easier. You can include anything in your outline you think will help.

---

*If you want more outlining ideas, Donald Murray has tucked a comprehensive treasury of outlining methods in the middle of his wonderful book *A Writer Teaches Writing* (a book all writing teachers should read).

OUTLINING METHODS (HANDOUT)

COLLECTION BOXES

For this method of outlining, divide the piece into several major categories, then collect your facts and ideas under each category.

EXAMPLE

Key idea: Owning a pet turtle

Category 1: Feeding Habits

Like leafy vegetables and bugs or worms

Prepared foods at pet store

Category 2: Types of turtles

Box turtles and common green turtles are swimming turtles

Terrapins are land turtles

Swimming turtles take more care than land turtles

Category 3: Where to get turtles

Pet stores

Veterinarians sometimes get pets people don't want

Call zoo information office

Collect them in the wild (only common types)

Fiction writers can use categories, such as *settings, characters, scene ideas,* etc. The purpose of making a collection is to store information and ideas where they are easy to find. It is especially useful when you have a lot of background research you will need to review as you write.

CRITICAL PIECES

To make this outline, write certain critical scenes or sections first, then fill the outline in around them using one of the other outlining methods. For example, you could write the conclusion, then use branching, designs, or collection to outline the rest of the piece. Fiction writers can write the scene with the high point or the end, then outline back to the beginning scene.

THE SLUGLINE

Newspaper reporters write the stories, but somebody else writes the titles or *headlines* for the stories. The printers use a temporary headline, called a *slug* to keep track of a story that doesn't yet have a title. A slug describes the story in no more than five words. "Man Bites Dog" is the classic example of a slug. It tells a whole story in just three words. You can plan your pieces or stories with slugs. Write one slug for the overall piece or story, then write slugs for each major section or scene.

EXAMPLE

Overall: <u>Turtles as Pets</u>

Section 1: Buying a Turtle

Section 2: Making Your Turtle a Home

Section 3: Feeding Your Turtle

SKETCHING

When artists plan a big painting, they do practice sketches of little parts of the painting first. You can plan your writing with practice sketches as well. Below are a few ideas of the types of things you can sketch:

Fiction

- Describe your main character walking down a hall, getting mad at something, talking with a friend, talking with a stranger, being frightened by something, or feeling enthusiastic about something.
- Describe a character looking at the setting of the story.

Nonfiction

- Pick any idea in your piece and look at it from two points of view. Explain why you agree with the idea, then explain why you disagree with the idea.
- Write a letter to your ideal reader explaining why he or she needs to read what you are going to write.
- Write a letter to your writing group explaining how and why you plan to organize your piece a certain way.
- What is the most important idea or piece of information you intend to write about? Why is it more important than some of the other ideas?
- Choose any idea, fact, or instruction in your piece and write an example.

CHAINING

Write one paragraph of your piece. Choose one sentence from that paragraph. Write it down to start your next paragraph, and write the next paragraph about that sentence. Keep chaining one paragraph to another until you have four or five paragraphs, then cross out the repeat sentences.

(Handout continues on page 66.)

Chaining is fun to do with a friend. You write the first paragraph; your friend chains on the next one; you write the third, and so forth.

EXAMPLE

Peanut butter and jelly sandwiches are good, but they are hard to make. The peanut butter rips up the bread, and the jelly dribbles out the edges and sticks to everything. The first time you make a peanut butter and jelly sandwich, keep a wet washrag close by. If you go slowly, you won't make a mess.

The peanut butter rips up the bread, and the jelly dribbles out the edges and sticks to everything. Peanut butter is made of ground-up peanuts. If the peanuts don't contain very much oil, the peanut butter doesn't flow onto the sandwich as well. Jelly, on the other hand, is mostly made of sugar and water. The water makes it flow out of the sandwich and the sugar is sticky when damp.

CUT AND PASTE

Sometimes, it's easiest just to get your ideas written down while they are fresh, then organize them later. In this outlining method, you outline after you write a rough draft. Write a rough draft of the whole piece from beginning to end. Then cut up with scissors what you've written and tape it down in a new order with tape. Fill in any missing sentences or rewrite sentences that don't fit anymore. You can use a design or any other outlining method to decide how to put it back together.

MIXED PLANS

You can mix and match your outlining methods. For example, you could break your story into major sections with sluglines, and then record all your ideas for that section with a branch.

Notes from the Pros:
On Fair Play

The old proverb—"teach the writer, not the writing"—is a good rule because writing doesn't always play fair. Despite enthusiasm and immense effort on the part of the writer, some pieces turn to spaghetti and some self-destruct. On the other hand, some seem to write themselves. It's not always clear why one piece won't settle down on the page or collapses altogether whereas others just flow. With writing, those who sweat most may achieve the poorest results. It isn't fair, but it is part of writing. Most writers have failed manuscripts languishing in the file cabinet.

Keep an eye on students. If one or two can't seem to make a piece work despite a long struggle, give them credit for their effort and a face-saving alternative. They've learned more than the others. Those who persist in the face of such disasters should always get credit for bravery. It's part of learning to try again after failing, and that's a big part of learning to write.

Notes from the Pros:
How Long Will It Take?

Students may be interested in knowing how long it takes a professional writer to write something. The man to consult is Lawrence Block. Block, in addition to writing novels, writes a column for *Writer's Digest Magazine* and teaches writing workshops. Block's book, *Writing the Novel from Plot to Print*, is one of the most practical, honest, and down-to-earth books on actually getting any book—not just a novel—written that we've run across. We recommend it for serious high school students who want to write a book. (Be aware, however, that Block is also honest about how he paid his dues by writing porn novels and why writing and drinking don't mix.) He got interested in writers' work habits and surveyed them. According to Block, most professionals average four to five pages a day, not counting research and planning or final editing and copyediting. From start to finish, a book a year—including time off between books—is a good output for a professional. That works out to something like one page a day. Then there's Isaac Asimov, who does fifty, but he is truly unique. Students may want to take another look at their planning. How long is this *really* going to take?

Chapter 3

Getting the Words to Flow on Paper

CHAPTER CONTENTS

Every nightmare (and even dogs have them) hints at the secret reserves of imaginative power in the human mind. What the stalled or not-yet-started writer needs is some magic for getting in touch with himself, some key.

— John Gardner

INTRODUCTION

Writing down a telephone message, directions to a friend's house, or the answer to a question on a test is not at all the same as writing a unified story, essay, or report—no more than painting a house is the same as painting a landscape. Drafting a complete piece is a whole new world.

When beginning writers first encounter this new world, the change is a shock. A person writing down a telephone message knows how long it will take to write it down and has a fair idea of what the result will be. Those writing longer pieces soon discover that sometimes they are hot, sometimes stone cold. They can not estimate whether a drafting session will go well, nor can they estimate how long it will take to finish a piece. They are haunted by a sense that the result could easily be an embarrassing catastrophe, understanding what Aldous Huxley meant when he said, "A bad book is as much of a labour to write as a good one; it comes as sincerely from the author's soul." Worse yet, they have trouble deciding how well it turned out once they have finished. This is not a problem for students alone. Working writers often remark that they don't know how a piece turned out, even though they have just reread it. Students may only have a vague sense that they have lost control. Writing suddenly feels like drifting helplessly on the sea in a glass float when it used to feel like rowing a boat. "I can't make my imagination work on time," wailed one student.

The rules are upside down in the new world. Puzzling out how to manage takes a long time, especially if no one mentions that it *is* a new world with different rules. Trying to cope under pressure leads a surprising number of students to suffer from writing blocks at an early age. Some find writing so painful that they refuse to try any more.

Avoiding Writing Blocks

The term *writer's block* brings to mind an agonized genius living in a cold sweat, unable to get one line on paper, not a seventh grader who scrawls out a few careless paragraphs and tosses the work at the teacher, never wanting to see it again. The fully blocked writer is indeed a rare phenomenon, but almost all those who write face a few garden-variety writing problems at one time or another:

1. They can't get started.

2. They can't find a voice for the piece, and it sounds stilted, phony, or cramped.

3. They write in painful fits and jerks.

4. They can only write occasionally.

5. They can't finish.

6. They suddenly lose confidence in their work.

7. They hit a wall about two-thirds of the way through.

As editor and writer Gene Fowler said, "Writing is easy; all you do is sit staring at a blank sheet of paper until the drops of blood form on your forehead." It is no joke. These obstacles cause more writing failures for students than anything else in writing. If students can't surmount them, all progress ends.

Writing isn't one task, but many different tasks combined. Some tasks require creativity, others objectivity. Unfortunately, it is nearly impossible to be creative and objective at once. These conflicts are the basic source of writing blocks. In order to help students separate conflicting writing chores, we tell them that learning to write in the new world is just like training two separate people to do different jobs. Writing will be much easier if students pretend that they have two people inside of them, taking turns working on the project.

This is not a new idea. One of the first writers to note the split nature of writing was Virgil. There has always been a creative side to writing and an editorial one. Over the centuries, writers have called the two sides of writing many things: "the creator and the critic," "the writer and the editor," "the unconscious and the conscious," "the right brain and the left brain." We call them the artist and the craftsman.*

The Artist's Job Description

The artist is in charge of imagination and drafting. Don't be confused by the term *artist* into thinking we are only discussing fiction. The artist drafts snappy business letters, clear lab reports, thoughtful commentaries, and winning legal briefs as well as riveting dialogue and vivid description. The artist supplies the basic materials of any written piece:

word flow	sentences	paragraphs
ideas	individuality	natural voice
rhythm	style	images
metaphors	analogies	observation
mood	whimsy	unity of thought
organizational unity	patterns	synthesis

---

*Female craftsmen tell us that they still prefer craftsman to craftswoman or craftsperson because the substitutes sound so clumsy—the very thing good craftsmen aren't. We bow to their choice at least in part because it provides such a good opportunity for discussing the evolution of language with students. Replacing words and style rules to reflect the equality of women is just one of many changes to the English language occurring today of which students should be aware.

The Craftsman's Job Description

The craftsman is in charge of organization and editing—a sort of business manager for the artist who organizes the work and later deals with the outside world. The craftsman:

- decides when, where, and how long the artist will write

- puts together plans

- analyzes and judges the drafts

- gives the artist suggestions for revision

- finds the proper detail or word when the artist's choice isn't quite right

- polishes and produces the final piece

- deals with teachers, editors, and readers

Happily, there are just two ground rules for writing free of blocks:

1. *Separate the artist from the craftsman.*

    The key to writing free of blocks is to separate the work of the artist from the work of the craftsman throughout the writing process. Each has a different set of jobs that should not be mixed. For example, never mix drafting and editing. Drafting needs word flow. It is a job for artists. Editing, on the other hand, requires judgment—a craftsman's task.

    Spelling, punctuation, vocabulary, and penmanship all belong to the craftsman and should never be considered during early drafts. Concern over them will slow down the drafting and break the artist's train of thought. On the other hand, setting up the work conditions is the craftsman's job. When the artist does it, it's called daydreaming, not writing.

    Leave time between doing the chores of the artist and those of the craftsman. For example, don't try to draft and edit in the same session. Don't even try to plan and draft in the same session. Beginners should leave at least twenty-four hours between tasks.

    Once students learn the two different sets of jobs, many like to give their personal artist and craftsman names to separate the two more clearly.

2. *Give the artist and the craftsman equal standing and train them to equal strength.*

    One is not "better" than the other. A weakness in one weakens both. If the craftsman becomes too strong, too critical, or interferes too soon, the artist is blocked. The words won't flow and there isn't much for the craftsman to prune and shape later. On the other hand, the artist is a bit lazy. Without the help of the craftsman, the piece may never be finished. Both the artist and the craftsman must be equally strong, working in harmony.

    There is a little artist in each of us. To tap into our creative powers, we only need to know one thing: *the artist is already there.* One of our students called his artist "The Force," tempting us to take the whole class to see *Star Wars.* Luke Skywalker finds his artist by simply learning to use The Force. He doesn't need to create The Force; he just needs to learn how to release it and then how to direct it. That is exactly how writers train their artists.

This chapter belongs to the artists in your students. Our first set of activities in this chapter — "Early Morning Freewrite," "Creative Concentration," and "Braindancing and Downhilling" — helps students release the artists within. The remaining activities help students begin to control and direct their artists. Be prepared to have fun, and try to make drafting class as magical as you can. The artist thrives on magic.

FREEING THE ARTIST

All activities in this section should be done in a practice journal or on scratch paper, so students aren't tempted to try the perfect first draft. Be sure they try braindancing and downhilling before they do the later activities.

Activity 1:
Early Morning Freewrite

If you are to have the full benefit of the richness of the unconscious, you must learn to write easily and smoothly when the unconscious is in the ascendant.

— Dorothea Brande

In her wonderful book *Becoming a Writer*, Dorothea Brande points out that the easiest way to release the artist is to write first thing in the morning. Although it is difficult to persuade students to do this regularly, this activity does noticeably improve the work of those who use the technique. Asking "how did the freewrites go this morning?" is also a pleasant way to open up a class discussion on writing problems.

Instructions to Students

Put your personal journal and a good free-flowing pen on the nightstand before you go to bed. Get up a few minutes earlier than usual, sit up in bed, and start writing before doing *anything* else — including brushing your teeth. Write about anything that happens to come to mind for a few minutes. Don't look at your writing. Just put it away.

After you have done this every day for a couple of weeks, we can talk about some of the neat things you'll find in your journal at one of our conferences. But don't look at it for a week or so. We'll give you a hint what you'll find when you do look: you'll find a lot of junk, but also some writing that is so terrific you won't believe you did it. We don't know why this happens. Somehow early in the morning, your artist is awake even though the rest of you is asleep. It's magic. After awhile, something else will start to happen, too. All the other writing you do will seem easier and turn out better. More magic.

Activity 2:
Creative Concentration

*What a release to write so that one forgets oneself, forgets
one's companion, forgets where one is or what one is going to
do next — to be drenched in sleep or in the sea. Pencils and
pads and curling blue sheets alive with letters heap up on the
desk.*

— Anne Morrow Lindbergh

Many people say that writing takes tough discipline. This is only partly true. What writing absolutely requies is focused concentration. Achieving that concentration requires discipline.

Because a writer who can't concentrate is in hopeless shape, this activity has become a ritual in our class. We do it together every drafting day and on many other days as well. It not only unfrazzles the frazzled and retrieves the energies of those who just got out of P.E., it also gives students a strong sense of being in a special group and teaches them how to concentrate when they need to write on their own.

Instructions to Students

The reason concentration is so important is that the artist comes out when you concentrate, but concentration is hard to force. "Concentrate!" you tell yourself clenching your fists. Sometimes it works. Often, it doesn't. There is another way to concentrate — the artist's way. We call it *creative concentration*. Think back to doing something you really enjoyed. Did you ever become so involved that you didn't notice the time or what was happening around you? That's creative concentration. It's a little like daydreaming, except you aren't just dreaming. You are *doing*. Creative concentration is the best kind of concentration for writing.

The steps to creative concentration are quite simple, but they are almost the opposite of clenching your fists and trying to force it.

1. Relax and clear your mind of other things.

2. Focus on what you want to write about.

3. Now that your concentration is focused, start writing and keep going without stopping for a little while until you are rolling.

Let's try each of these steps together while we explain.

STEP 1.   Relax and clear your mind of other things.

For most people, the best time to write is usually early in the morning because they are relaxed and don't have other things on their minds yet. At other times it helps to know how to deliberately relax and clear your mind. There are many ways to do this. Let's try an easy way that works for most people:

- First, relax your muscles. You can't clear your mind if the rest of you is tense or wiggling around. Take a good stretch. Cats are experts at stretching. Stretch like a cat. Stretch all your muscles. Lift your shoulders up to touch the bottom of your ears, then let them drop. Stretch your arms as far as you can. Still stretched, move them around in a big circle. Clasp your hands behind your back and then bend over, stretching your arms up.

- Sit down and close your eyes. Starting with your feet and working up to the top of your head, tense your muscles as tight as you can. Tense them a little more, then suddenly relax.

- Next, take deep breaths. With your arms and legs uncrossed and your eyes closed, take a deep breath. Slowly breathe out. Take another. Slowly breathe out. Taking a few deep breaths is nature's way of relaxing people. It puts oxygen in people's systems, and that's relaxing.

- Clear your mind of other thoughts. Sit very still with your eyes closed and picture a wall painted all one color. If some thought drifts into your mind, gently push it aside and picture the color again. Keep returning to the color of the wall. Pretty soon, you will be able to think about the color without a lot of other thoughts. You want your mind to be still before you start the next step.

STEP 2. Focus on what you want to write about.

Think about the characters, an interesting fact, the first sentence, or anything else about the piece you want to write. Just let the thoughts about it float into your head. Don't try to organize them. After a couple of minutes, think about what you might write down first. Pretty soon, you'll be ready to start writing.

STEP 3. Start writing and keep going without stopping.

Start writing and write for at least three to five minutes without stopping. If you can't think what to say, write "I can't think what to say." You don't need to write fast, you don't go back to make changes or corrections. The point is to start gently and then keep writing without stopping. It won't take long before you are rolling. It is a little like starting a car by rolling it down a hill. That first five minutes is your first push to get your writing car rolling. If you like braindancing (see next activity), braindance for at least five minutes without stopping, then downhill for another five.

Activity 3:
Braindancing and Downhilling

True ease in writing comes from art, not chance
As those move easiest who have learned to dance.
—Alexander Pope

This method of persuading the words to flow has many names. Gabriele Rico calls it *clustering* and *webbing* in her book *Writing the Natural Way*, which explores using a similar method with many different kinds of writing. We used to call it *brainstorming* and *fast-writing*, but students would choose Wagnerian-sized themes and write like a sprinter heading for the tape. The process is much lazier: let ideas dance to mind, record them quickly, and then slip gracefully down the page like an expert downhill skier—*braindancing* and *downhilling.*

This activity, a student favorite, is especially helpful for those who find the physical mechanics of expressing a thought in a sentence so slow that they lose the thought before they finish the sentence.

Students enjoy using different colored pens and pencils to braindance. Some people have an incredible urge to make their writing look pretty; in a first draft, they should not. Using pretty colors to braindance satisfies this urge, removing the pressure they feel to draft beautifully (and perfectly) the first time.

Braindancing and downhilling work best with poems, short pieces, or short sections of longer works.

Instructions to Students

Writing is thinking on paper. Have you ever gotten in the middle of writing something and forgotten what you were planning to say? As you write longer and longer pieces, you will bump into this little problem more often. Everybody does, because thinking is fast, but writing is slow. Learning to hold a thought in your mind until you get it on paper takes practice.

Braindancing helps you remember your thoughts, and downhilling helps you get them down on paper. Recording thoughts in a braindance takes two minutes. Writing them out in sentences takes ten. Drafting the actual story may take several hours.

There's another reason braindancing makes writing easier. People often think of the end of a story before they think of the beginning. When you braindance, you can record your thoughts in the order they come to you and then write about them in any order you wish.

Before you start, take a tip from us: get organized first.

1. Get our several pens and pencils and several sheets of notebook paper before you begin. You don't want to break your concentration by hunting around for pens or paper after you've started.

2. Write on one side of the page using every other line. If you decide to edit later on, it'll be a lot more work if you don't leave space for it now. You also won't be able to cut and paste if you've written on both sides of the page.

3. Leave big margins. Using a ruler or a straightedge, draw a line down several of the pages you will use for downhilling. Leave a three-inch margin on the right-hand side of each page and lightly draw a big *X* on the back. This will help you remember to leave space and to write on just one side of the page.

4. Pick a writing idea before you begin. You can also choose an idea for a section or a scene of a longer piece. Just be sure you decide what to write about ahead of time.

How to Braindance

The process of braindancing involves the following steps:

STEP 1.   Record your writing idea.

On a clean sheet of paper write a word or a phrase in capital letters in the middle of the page. Draw a circle around it. This word or phrase represents your writing idea (or at least a starting point). If you are working on a section of a longer piece, it represents your idea for that section.

If you can't think of an idea, use *breakfast* this time. Almost everyone can think of something to say about breakfast.

STEP 2.   Develop creative concentration (see activity 2).

STEP 3.   Record your thoughts as they come to you.

To record a thought, just write down a couple of words that will help you remember the thought later on. For example, suppose you are writing a story about a dog, and one of your thoughts is "this

dog chews pink tennis shoes." You could record it by writing (dog) or (dog shoes) or (pink shoes).

If you forgot the thought later on, just looking at these words would remind you.

Put a circle around each thought after you record it. The circle around the words is important. It separates one thought from another and makes each thought easier to remember. Draw lines between thoughts that you think are connected. Your paper ends up looking like a little spiderweb of your thoughts.

Don't try hard and don't hurry. Also, don't try to decide if the thoughts are good or not. Just let the thoughts come and record them—whatever they are. Record thoughts that you may not use to write, as well as those you may use. You will never use all the thoughts in your braindance to write. On the other hand, if you record all your thoughts, you won't run short of thoughts and run out of things to say. See if you can fill the page with thoughts.

EXAMPLE (*Note to teachers:* A quick way to demonstrate braindancing is to ask students to call out ideas as you record them on the blackboard or on an overhead.)

Writing Idea: A story about a stubborn dog named Harry.

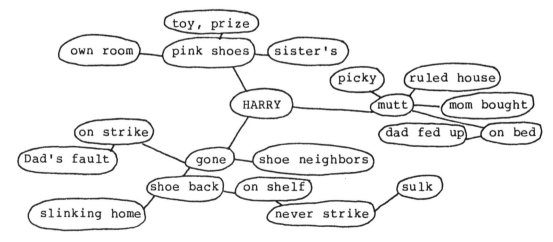

Below are some of the thoughts written out in sentences:

"Harry was a mutt that Mom brought home one day. Harry soon tried to rule the whole house. He was picky too. He insisted on having his own room. He took a pink tennis shoe from my sister's closet and wouldn't give it back. It was his toy, his prize. Finally, when Harry decided to sleep on Dad's bed, Dad got fed up and tried to boot him off. The next morning Harry was gone. And so was his shoe...."

How to Downhill

Pick one thought on your braindance as a place to start and start writing. Don't hurry. Just write like you are an expert skier gliding gently down the slope. Keep writing until you get to the end of your piece. If you are writing a long piece, write a section or a scene in one downhill swoop.

It's very important to keep going. Don't erase or cross out or back up. Fiddling with details and backing up is like skiing uphill. Besides taking a lot of energy, it doesn't work. Fix details and problems later. You want to feel free and easy when you downhill.

Further Tips on Braindancing and Downhilling

The following points will help you use these techniques:

- If you constantly slow down because you can't remember a word, a spelling, or a punctuation rule, don't skip over it. Make your best guess, mark it with an "unsure code," and then move on. Unsure codes help you find problems again, so you can fix them when you edit. Print the unsure codes in capital letters and put parentheses around them, so that they will be easy to see when you edit. You can make up your own codes. Here are the ones we like to use:

  (SP) = check spelling.

  (PUNCT) = check punctuation.

  (WORD) = find a better word.

  (FACT) = double check this fact.

  (CHECK _____) = Check whatever is noted in the blank space.

- If you think of something for another part of the piece, don't wait. You'll forget it. Record it on your braindance or add it in the margins drawing an arrow to the place it should go. You can also write your additions on a separate sheet of paper. Label them with different numbers, such as "ADD #1" or "ADD #2." Note where it should go by writing "ADD #1" at the place where you want to insert it.

- When you are drafting, you may sometimes bump into something Henriette Klauser calls *THE WALL*. This is just a place where you get stuck. Writers know it very well. Here's the trick: never stop writing at the wall. Plod along one sentence at a time for awhile. Tell yourself that you will keep writing for five more minutes. The wall doesn't go on forever. If you keep plodding, you will suddenly go right over the wall and breeze on through to the end.

- Go back and add to your braindance until you feel like writing again.

• If you must stop because you've run out of time, pick up the next time by braindancing some more. You might also try recopying the last paragraph and then continuing your downhill. Some writers like to edit their previous drafts as a way to get back into writing. You can try this, but most beginners find it easier to save editing until they have everything down on paper.

Activity 4:
Finding a Writing Place

The place isn't important. The color of ink or typewriter ribbon isn't important. The fancy files behind your desk or table aren't important. Not being distracted from turning out a page or more a day is important.

— Robert Aldeman

Writing takes a tremendous amount of concentration. Most writers aid concentration by choosing a particular place and time to use *daily* for writing. They can be fanatic about it, especially those who write books. Stories abound of writers who could not finish a book because their favorite restaurants closed or because they remodelled their offices and couldn't concentrate in the new ones. Most writers of books are also suspicious of stopping, even for a weekend. Many say they grow cold if they don't write at least every other day.

Students are not writing books, of course, but daily practice in a specified place at a specified time makes a world of difference to their writing. Writing is like playing the piano or golf: the only way to learn to do it is to practice, practice, practice.

Instructions to Students

You won't always have time in school to do all your writing, so your first homework assignment is to find at least one good place to write outside school. Professional writers notice which places are best for writing. Once they find a good place, they try to go there to write every day at the same time. They do this to help their concentration. Having a good writing place will make writing a lot easier. There is no particular place that works for everybody, but there are a few basic rules:

RULE 1.   No distractions.

Talking and writing don't mix. If the words come out of your mouth, they won't flow from your pen. Avoid places where other people interrupt you. Avoid places where others talk near you. Avoid places where you will want to talk yourself. Even pieces of paper or books on your desk can be distracting. Avoid messy places, cramped places, or places where you can't move distracting things out of your field of vision. Find a place that doesn't have too many things around to distract you.

Some people find *too much* quiet distracting. They like a little background noise. The trick is to make that noise boring. Foot-tapping music and interesting television programs will distract you. Very soft, slow music might be fine. You can buy tapes and records of the sounds of nature: birds, waterfalls, raindrops, etc. These work very well as nondistracting background noise.

RULE 2.   Same time, same place.

Always go to your writing place when you want to write or study. Try to find a place you can use at the same time every day. You will also want to avoid doing other things there. It's your writing place. You need to save it for concentration.

RULE 3.   Keep your materials together.

It's best to store your materials at the writing place. If not, you will need to remember to take your writing ideas notebook, practice journal, pens, pencils, paper, yesterday's drafts, and anything else you might need with you. If you can't keep them at your writing place, find a place where you can keep them all together.

RULE 4.   Notice what helps and what doesn't.

As you use your writing place, notice the things that help you and the things that distract you. Experiment to make your writing place a good, helpful place. Keep notes on ideas you have to make your writing place better. One other reminder: Make a habit of getting organized before you start writing. You want to concentrate on writing, not on finding things.

Now that you know what kinds of places are good, make a list of places near home or school where you could go to write. Don't forget the library. Tonight show the rules to your parents and ask them to help you find such a place. Tomorrow show your list to another teacher and ask for his or her suggestions. Bring your list with you tomorrow. We'll discuss the place and time you have chosen and work out any problems you might have.

Activity 5:
Between Friends

As a rule, what is out of sight disturbs men's minds more seriously than what they see.
— Julius Caesar

Anxiety about the topic, the genre, or some other feature of the writing is perhaps the chief obstacle to writing. It produces both an inability to get started and an inability to finish. This odd little exercise in which the writer has a heart-to-heart chat with the source of the anxiety is useful as a jump-start for students who are anxious about the assignment.

This activity does not work well in a group, although it can be done in pairs. Please note, your students may say, "huh?" when you first present this exercise. Try it yourself on some starting point that you feel anxious about before you launch the exercise on a class.

Instructions to Students

When you are worried about a writing assignment, it sometimes helps to hold a written conversation with the assignment itself.

To do this, first pick a writing idea, a starting point, or anything else about the writing that you want to think about. Then make your writing idea or starting point into an imaginary person to whom you can talk. Ask your starting point a question by writing down one of the questions we've put on the blackboard. Then pretend that you are the starting point and write down an answer. Keep asking questions and answering them. Hold a little question-and-answer conversation with your starting point about at least three of the questions on the handout.

Yes, this exercise is somewhat odd at first because you must pretend to be yourself and the imaginary person. But that's kind of fun, too. Just let your imagination run wild. Doing the exercise will help you get started writing the piece.

BETWEEN FRIENDS (HANDOUT)

Questions to make your starting point (or writing idea) into someone or something to whom you can talk:

1. What do you look like? A person? Something else? How tall are you? Skinny or fat? How are you dressed?

2. Where do you come from? When did you start? When did I first meet you?

3. Do I like you? Why do I like you? Why don't I like you?

4. Do you help people? What ways do you help people?

5. Are you ever mean to people? How are you mean to people?

6. What is the most interesting thing about you? the least interesting? What is the strangest thing about you?

Questions to help you get to know the starting point or writing idea better:

7. What do I know about you?

8. What don't I know about you?

9. What have I read about you? seen in movies or on television?

10. Who is most interested in you? Why are they interested?

11. What is the one word that best describes you?

12. What is the best thing that ever happened because of you? the worst?

13. Have you changed recently? How?

14. What would I most like to know about you?

Questions to help you understand your feelings about the starting point:

15. What can writing about you do for me?

16. If you were a good friend and could tell me one thing about yourself, what would that be?

17. What is the biggest problem I have with writing about you?

18. What could I do to make writing about you easier?

19. What would help me get started writing about you?

20. How will talking with you like this help me write about you?

21. Is there anything else that I should know about you?

22. (Make up your own question to ask the starting point or writing idea.)

Notes from the Pros:
On Talking about It

Many books on teaching writing suggest (as we do) that students talk about what they are going to write while they plan, but the professionals tend to share Norman Mailer's view: "It's hard to talk about one's present work, for it spoils something at the root of the creative act. It discharges tension."

Some students may also feel that talking about their work makes drafting more difficult for them, even though others find talking helpful. The middle course may be best. Encourage students to discuss the possibilities for a piece before they draft. Discuss the piece with them during drafting only if they have a problem. Once they have an idea of a solution, send them back to the desk, saying, "Don't tell me, write it down."

Teacher's Notebook: On
Remembering Writing

By the time we write our last research paper and leave college, we all tend to anchor our writing to shore and never cast out to sea again. It's easy to forget what we ask of students when most of our own writing is telephone messages, grocery lists, and notes to parents.

For many students—especially those still struggling with spelling or the mechanics of holding the pen—writing may seem about as natural as learning to swing a golf club. You may be out of touch with this feeling if you haven't recently held a long club in a miserably uncomfortable grip and tried to swing smoothly as you bend your knees, keep your head still, shift your weight, don't raise your hip, keep your left arm straight, and remember which direction you are hitting the ball. "Relax!" says the coach. It's a wonder more golf coaches aren't clubbed to death. Writing students have similar thoughts about their teachers.

It's much easier to teach students to write if you are grappling with writing something yourself, even if it's only a few early-morning thoughts in a personal journal. Write with your students. It's good for them to see adults do it. Set aside your writing time in class and teach students to respect the privacy of those who are trying to write by insisting that they not interrupt you.

If you can't think of anything to write about, look over the class and pick any student. Write a little scene sketching a moment in the classroom with your student: the setting, what you said, how you felt. Don't pick a big moment, pick a little one, as small as a glance.

Set aside a Saturday morning to go to the library, a local cafe, or even the airport for a few hours of uninterrupted drafting. Write about what it felt like to draft stories on your own. Share your observations with your students.

If you start writing yourself, one thing you will notice is that concentrated drafting is exhausting. Three or four hours is about the maximum an adult can handle during a day. In class, you'll always find at least one student who won't have enough energy to write that day. Be sure to develop writing classroom jobs, such as overseeing the reference books, typing, copyediting, drawing illustrations, making book covers, or taking care of the background tapes. Assign these jobs to students who are too worn out to write.

DIRECTING THE ARTIST

Students must know how to use braindancing and downhilling and also must have some confidence with just letting the words flow on paper to use the activities in this section. These are not one-time activities but favorites we haul out regularly to inspire students to draft more easily.

Activity 6:
Zoom Lens

The oldest books are still only just out to those who have not read them.

—Samuel Butler

Nature designed six-year-olds to write delightful poetry and eighteen-year-olds to write passionate opinions. It designed twelve- to fifteen-year-olds to write fiction. Their desire to get to the heart of the action, keen observation of detail, and strong emotions are all advantages in fiction. Teachers are always a little surprised by this observation because so much of the writing they see from students is flat and clichéd. In part, this is natural. A cliché is a good metaphor that has been overused, but it is still new to young people. In their eyes it is as fresh and funny as the day it was coined. Nevertheless, they need to work on using fewer clichés to write.

Some teachers try to help students by requiring them to use more adjectives and adverbs. We've tried this ourselves, but it usually produces rather strange pieces littered with words a good editor would cut. We have switched to "Zoom Lens," which helps students avoid clichés by making the most of their natural talents.

Instructions to Students

Today we are going to practice "Zoom Lens." This writing exercise comes from a favorite rule of writers: *Show, Don't Tell.* The zoom lens not only makes drafting easier, but it also makes your stories more fun to read because it helps you find interesting details so that you can *show* your reader the characters or settings instead of *telling* your reader about them.

Suppose you are describing a character named Mr. Brown. You could write "Mr. Brown was nice." This is not very interesting. It doesn't show us anything about Mr. Brown. "Mr. Brown was wonderfully nice" or "Mr. Brown was charming" are not much better. Readers like details. You want to *show* your reader what your characters are like; *don't tell* your reader about them. In other words, show Mr. Brown doing nice things, don't just say he was nice.

EXAMPLE (describing a character)

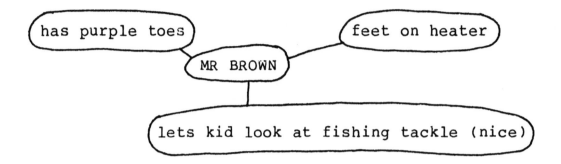

Mr. Brown had purple toes. He ran a small hardware store in town, the kind of store that had one of just about everything. Sunday afternoons, when business was slow, he'd sit up front and let me wander through the store. My favorite section was the fishing tackle. I'd gloat over every new spinner and weight, dreaming that some day I could actually buy one. He'd take off his shoes and socks and put his feet right on top of the small electric heater he kept by the cash register. I asked him once why his feet didn't burn.

"See them toes?" he said. "They're purple, cold as ice all winter. Can't get 'em warmed up enough to burn."

See how much more interesting Mr. Brown is when the writer shows Mr. Brown being nice? In the course of describing Mr. Brown, the example told quite a lot of the story, too. The reader knows the story takes place in a small town and also meets the character of the kid who likes to look at fishing tackle in Mr. Brown's store.

How to Play Zoom Lens

STEP 1.   Create a picture of a character in your mind. Put your character in a place—the setting.

STEP 2.   Pretend to be a camera operator filming the scene. Look at your scene through the camera.

STEP 3.   Once you have the scene set in your mind, zoom in on at least three details about what your character looks like, what your character is doing, or how your character is feeling.

STEP 4.   Use the details from step 3 to write a paragraph or two describing the character and/or the setting.

Get out your practice journal and try it yourself.

The zoom lens also helps you describe settings. Normally, you don't describe the setting all at once. You describe it a little at a time as the action of the story takes place. Suppose you want to describe part of the setting by describing a character looking at the sunset. You could write "the sky was beautiful" or you could use the zoom lens to show your reader details.

EXAMPLE (describing a setting)

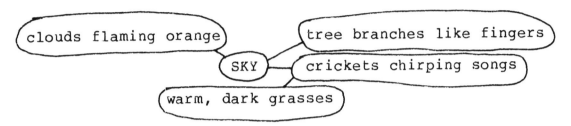

Joe stared at the setting sun watching the clouds flame orange and melt soft pink. The trees stood in a row along the crest of the hill, black-fingered branches dancing with a gentle joy to the songs of crickets in the warm, dark grass.

"I can never leave this place," he sighed.

See how much better a reader can picture the sunset? Now try describing a setting yourself in your practice journal.

If you are having a hard time getting a scene in your mind, try making up at least three details for each of the five senses. Start with something simple, such as "girl sitting on a rock." Pretend you're the girl. Make up at least three details describing how it smells, tastes, feels, sounds, and looks to be sitting on that rock. Top it off by imagining how your character feels at that moment. You probably won't use all the details you create, but you'll have plenty of ideas.

EXAMPLE (using the five senses)

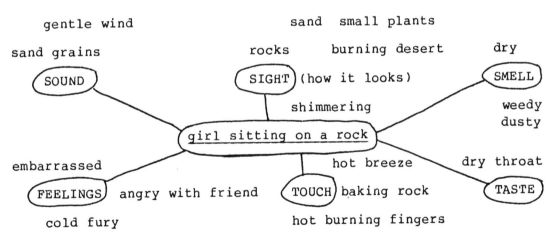

Mary crouched down and tested the warmth of the rock with her fingertips before settling on it. She stared across miles of shimmering rock and sand. Usually the dusty smell and the gentle press of the hot breeze calmed her. But not today. Today, the desert brought with it cold fury.

Try using the five senses to write a description of either a character or a setting in your practice journal.

Have you ever said, "I'm bored"? Well, this one is just for you. You can use the zoom lens to help you describe a character's mood, such as *bored*, *happy*, or *frightened*. For example, picture yourself in a place that is boring. Use the zoom lens to pick out at least three details of the scene. Use the five senses to get more details, if you wish. Then write a couple of paragraphs of a story about a character being bored *without using the words bored or boring*.

The list of words below are good clues that it's time to try the zoom lens. They tend to pop up next to *was* (or *is*) when you are telling, not showing.

TELL WORDS

About Characters	About Settings
was nice	was beautiful
was pretty (or beautiful)	was warm
was ugly	was cold
was friendly	was dark
was sad	was sunny
was bored	was scary
was weird	was strange
was interesting	was spooky
was dumb	was boring
was lazy	was weird
was funny	was empty
was terrific	was dirty
was smart	was wet
was a pain in the neck	
was tall, dark, and handsome	

Additional Notes to Teachers

Make a practice of collecting dull adjectives and clichés from your students' pieces to add to the tell words list.

Activity 7:
Hooks and Leaders

Beginning a book is unpleasant.... Worse than not knowing your subject is not knowing how to treat it, because that's finally everything.

—Phillip Roth

Many students can't get started because they have so much trouble writing the first sentence. This exercise provides them with some first sentence models to help them over the hump.

Instructions to Students

You want your opening to grab your reader's attention and then make your reader want to keep reading. The first couple of sentences are worth some special attention.

It helps to think of your opening as two sentences: *the hook* to grab your reader's attention and *the leader* to carry him into the piece. Just like a fishing line. The hook grabs the fish; the leader drags it into the boat. What hooks a reader? Information, surprises, or suspense. What leads the reader on? Knowing a little bit more about what is to come, but not everything. In fiction, the leader sets up a little puzzle to be solved by further reading. In nonfiction, the leader promises more information for the reader who keeps reading.

You can write your hook and leader any time. Some writers put down anything for a first sentence just to get started. Then they rewrite the opening after they finish the rest of the piece. Others like to have the opening written before they start drafting. Either way, it helps to try several different openings, then pick the one that you like best.

There are thousands of different kinds of hooks and leaders. In the "Hooks and Leaders Handout" we've listed ten different kinds of hooks to give you some ideas.

Let's look at two of them in detail: the *shocker* and the *summary* hooks. We need a writing idea to start. Let's pretend that we want to write a fantasy story about a girl and a dragon. We'll name the girl Jesse. Fantasies often have magicians, many of them named Merlin. We like magicians, so we'll make one up—Marlon the Magician. (We are quite sure you can come up with more creative names, but these names will do for now.)

First, we'll write a shocker hook. The shocker hook is based on surprising the reader. This hook begins with a life or death (or at least dangerous) situation. Then we'll add a leader that creates a little suspense. (The hook is in italics. The rest is the leader.)

EXAMPLE (fiction shocker hook)

A purple dragon can change your life or squash you flat. When Marlon sent the dragon to Jesse, he couldn't be sure which would happen. He just hoped for the best.

Not bad. The shocker presents a scary choice: change or get squashed. The leader gives the reader a puzzle. We learned that Marlon sent the dragon, but we don't know everything. If dragons are so dangerous, why did he send it? Does he hate Jesse? No. The next sentence says he hoped for the best. He's worried. He obviously was forced to send the dragon, but we don't know why or what will happen unless we keep reading.

The summary hook grabs the reader with information. It tells the reader who, what, when, where, why, and how in one sentence. Again, we'll use a leader that creates a little mystery or some suspense.

EXAMPLE (fiction summary hook)

      (who)   (what)   (how)   (where)   (when)
When Jesse saw the purple dragon appear in the meadow one Friday, she knew Marlon the

    (why)
Magician had sent it. Marlon always sent something on Friday, and it usually caused trouble.

      In this example, the leader actually creates several little mysteries. Why should Marlon send things to Jesse? What is their relationship? Why on Friday? Is this dragon going to cause trouble? What kind? Read on to find out!

Hooks and leaders help with nonfiction first sentences too. We need an idea to start. Let's pick "why people should buckle their seatbelts" and try shocker and summary hooks and leaders.

EXAMPLE (nonfiction shocker hook)

If you don't buckle up this morning, you could be dead by noon. If people knew the facts, they would buckle up more often.

EXAMPLE (nonfiction summary hook)

                           (where—in your car)

    (who)   (how)   (what)
Each time you buckle your seatbelt, you reduce your chances of being killed or injured

  (when)
that day by 50 percent. Why do people who try to protect themselves in other ways so often fail to buckle up?

This example tells who, what, why, when, where, and how about an interesting fact. The leader promises information about why people don't buckle up. For those of you who have worked with the prewriting choices, notice that the leader in nonfiction often leads into the piece by presenting your key idea.

Now you need to practice writing some hooks and leaders. Choose a writing idea and try writing at least three different hoods and leaders for the story. Use the hook and leader handout for ideas. Choose the hook and leader you think turned out best.

HOOKS AND LEADERS (HANDOUT)

There are as many first sentences as there are stories and writers. You might like to collect the first sentences of other writers. Study them. Write your own versions. See how they did it. In this handout, we have ten different types of hooks.

You will probably notice that our hooks and leaders get you off to a fast start. Longer pieces and more academic pieces often have more leisurely openings. These are just ten ideas to help you when you are stuck. If a good first sentence comes to you naturally, use that one.

1. SHOCKER: The shocker hook opens the story with a life or death (or at least dangerous) situation.

   Fiction example: *A purple dragon can change your life or squash you flat.* When Marlon sent the dragon to Jesse, he couldn't be sure which would happen. He just hoped for the best.

   Nonfiction example: *If you don't buckle up this morning, you could be dead by noon.* If people knew the facts, they would buckle up more often.

2. SUMMARY: The summary hook tells the reader who, what, when, where, why, and how in one compact sentence.

   Fiction example: *When Jesse saw the purple dragon appear in the meadow one Friday, she knew Marlon the Magician had sent it.* Marlon always sent something on Friday, and it usually caused trouble.

   Nonfiction example: *Each time you buckle your seatbelt, you reduce your chances of being killed or injured that day by 50 percent.* Seatbelts have saved more lives in the past twenty years than any other human invention.

3. CAPSULE: The capsule hook jumps right in with a brief wrap-up or a shorter summary than the full summary hook.

   Fiction example: *Marlon the Magician sent something every Friday, and it usually caused trouble; the purple dragon was no exception.* Jesse, of course, didn't know it, but this particular purple dragon was sent to save her life.

   Nonfiction example: *Seatbelts have saved more lives in the past twenty years than any other human invention.* Even more lives can be saved if we take a few seconds to buckle up each time we get in a car.

4. DEFINITION: The definition hook begins with a real definition from the dictionary, or—better yet—one you make up.

   Fiction example: *Dragons are huge, terrifying beasts with beautiful, jewelled eyes and disgusting breath. The friendly ones are purple.* It was the purple variety that met Jesse in a meadow one Friday.

   Nonfiction example: *A seatbelt is something you spend three seconds buckling to save three years in the hospital.* The simple act of buckling up each time you get in a car reduces your chances of getting injured or killed by 50 percent.

(Handout continues on page 92.)

5. PROBLEM: The problem hook briefly suggests a problem that you are going to solve in the piece.

Fiction example: *If a large purple dragon drops into a meadow in front of you one day, it won't go away until you understand why it came.* Jesse knew Marlon had sent the dragon, but she hadn't the faintest idea why.

Nonfiction example: *Most people's biggest driving problem is getting their passengers to buckle up.* The best way to accomplish this life-saving task is to explain the facts.

6. QUESTION: The question hook asks a question that you intend to answer in the piece.

Fiction example: *The problem for Jesse was this: what do you do with a large, purple dragon?* Hers landed in a meadow in front of her one Friday afternoon. Obviously Marlon had sent it, but she had no idea why.

Nonfiction example: *Before you start your car, do you check to be certain all your passengers are buckled up?* You can save money, time, and grief with a two-second check.

7. STATEMENT OF AUTHORITY: The statement of authority hook is most often used by experts writing on their subject of expertise. You can use it too, provided you show why you are an expert.

Fiction example: *When Marlon sends you a purple dragon, he has a good reason.* I know. He sent me one, and it caused no end of trouble. (In this case the expert is Jesse.)

Nonfiction example: *According to a survey I took of students in my school, only 30 percent of them buckle their seatbelts every time they get into a car.* They might buckle up more often if they knew the facts. (You are the expert because you did the survey.)

8. QUOTATION: The quotation hook begins with a quote from a real person or from a book, magazine, or newspaper. Just make sure it fits your story or subject. For fiction, you can make up books, magazines, or newspapers to quote.

Fiction example: *"In 3050 King Fardmen declared the last dragon dead."—The History of the House of Fardmen.* Jesse had read the famous history of her country written by the scholar Quiliman, and she knew it was wrong, particularly on the subject of dragons. One Friday, over 150 years after the King declared dragons extinct, a large, purple dragon appeared before her. Dead? No. This dragon was most certainly alive, at least lively enough to cause her no end of trouble.

Nonfiction example: *"I know I should wear seatbelts, but I often don't," said Bill Bramer, a student at Leschi Middle School.* According to my survey, Bill is like many students at Leschi. Over 70 percent of those surveyed said they often failed to buckle their seatbelts.

9. STATISTICS: This statistics hook cites a statistic that leads into the piece.

Fiction example: *According to the Fardmen Daily Screamer, over 80 percent of all dragon sightings in the year 4101 were somehow connected with one man, the Magician named Marlon.* Experts claimed this statistic was pure twaddle. They maintained that both the Magician Marlon and dragons were myths. Jesse never believed in the magician, but the day a large, purple dragon appeared before her, she knew Marlon had sent it.

Nonfiction example: *One in every eight people will be involved in an automobile accident at least once in their lives.* Even a minor fender-bender can produce serious injuries if the passengers are not wearing seatbelts.

10. COMPARISON OR CONTRAST: The comparison or contrast hook compares two things for similarities, contrasts their differences, or both.

Fiction example (contrasting girls to dragons): *Young, headstrong girls and dragons have little in common. Girls can rarely be successfully ordered around, whereas dragons are always under orders, usually those of a magician. Girls laugh at magicians; dragons worship them. Girls are sometimes pretty; dragons are always gorgeous, if you can ignore their stink.* Getting a girl together with a dragon is difficult, but this was the Magician Marlon's task one Friday when he sent a large, purple dragon to meet a girl named Jesse.

Nonfiction example (contrasting the use of thirty seconds): *It takes thirty seconds to buckle the average seatbelt and the same amount of time to die without one.* People who do not use seatbelts are twice as likely to die in an accident as those who do.

Activity 8:
Warm-ups for *Cold* Days

You don't start with any aesthetic manifesto,
you just do what works.
—E. L. Doctorow

Writing does wax hot and cold. Students, like all other writers, may have trouble starting because they are writing *cold* that day. We've collected a list of warm-up ideas to help students get started on cold days. You can just pass these along in a handout, although students often enjoy doing some of them as stand-alone activities in their practice journals.

Instructions to Students

When you start writing every day or every other day, you will begin to notice something strange about writing. Some days writing is very easy—you are writing *hot*. Nothing can stop you. Other days are just the opposite—you are writing *cold*, and it is harder to get started. There is nothing wrong with you; that is the way of writing.

You should not stop writing just because you are having a cold day. What you need to do is get warmed up. We have a handout listing some ideas for warming up on cold days. Save it. It's a very handy list.

WARM-UPS (HANDOUT)

- Concentrate on following your writer's routine. Don't worry about the deadline or the whole piece, just worry about the little part that you want to write today.

- Try to write badly. In her book, *Writing down the Bones*, Natalie Goldberg calls this *composting*. Gardeners compost old leaves and vegetable matter in order to prepare the garden soil. You are preparing to write the piece later by writing garbage now.

- Tell yourself that you will keep working for five more minutes. Then, if it's still going badly, you can try something else.

- Work on two pieces at the same time. If you are cold on one, switch to the other.

- Pick another section of the piece and start there. If you are stuck on the beginning, write the ending or the high point.

- Change your tools. Switch to a different pen. Try writing on a little bitty pad of paper. Try a great big art pad with big bright pens. Type the story on a computer with the screen switched off. Tell your story to a tape recorder.

- Draw a picture of your story, then write about it.

- Edit and recopy a section you have already drafted.

- Try Braindancing and Downhilling, Zoom Lens, Between Friends, Hooks and Leaders, or Follow the Leader.

- Hold a conference with your teacher or a member of your writing group. Try to explain why you are having trouble and get their suggestions.

- Pretend that you are someone else writing on the same subject. If you are writing about a porcupine, pretend to be the porcupine. If you are writing a romance, pretend to be a Martian anthropologist writing a letter home explaining it.

- Write about whatever is in front of you. Close your eyes, turn your head, and open your eyes again. Describe whatever you see in detail. Then describe the things around it. Once you have warmed up, start writing your main piece using that description. For example, suppose you describe a crack in the linoleum as a warm-up. Go back to your main story and write a section where one of your characters is looking at a crack in the linoleum.

- Try writing your piece in a different genre. Write your essay as a song, your story as a how-to, your film script as a poem, your news article as a short story, or your personal experience as a letter.

- Braindance backwards. Draw a pretty web of circles and lines without the thoughts filled in. Then go fill them in with whatever ideas seem appropriate.

- Forget that you are writing about anything. Just start writing and keep writing. Don't even try to write sentences. Write words or thoughts or feelings. Just write anything at all.

- Write backwards. Write the last sentence of a paragraph, then the sentence preceding it, then the sentence preceding that, working back to the beginning.

- Borrow a few words to start a first sentence.

EXAMPLE

I remember …

You wouldn't think that …

I have never …

For the past two years, I …

The last time I …

If you have never …

You think you know how to _____ until you …

A good friend can …

This morning was the first time I …

If you are writing fiction, you may prefer to translate these sentence-starters into the third person past tense.

EXAMPLE

He (or she) remembered …

He (or she) never dreamed that …

He (or she) had never …

- Make a connection to something totally unconnected and write about that. Suppose you are writing about the American Revolution. Look around you. How are the things you see connected to the American Revolution? For example, how are your tennis shoes connected to the American Revolution? Come up with any old idea on how they might be connected, and use your connection as a first sentence of a warm-up paragraph or two. Go ahead! Be ridiculous.

EXAMPLE

How are tennis shoes connected to the American Revolution?

The tennis shoe was invented to help Daniel Boone cross the Cumberland Gap.

EXAMPLE

How are fluorescent lights connected to the American Revolution?

Ben Franklin snapped on the fluorescent light and then …

(Handout continues on page 96.)

● Make up a starter sentence. Fold a piece of paper in half lengthwise. On the first half write a list of subjects (human, animal, vegetable, mineral, or any other noun). On the second half write a list of unusual verbs. A thesaurus or a dictionary can suggest words. (Don't be afraid to choose verbs you don't yet know; just be sure to look them up.) Open the paper, so that the subjects and the verbs are lined up. Write a sentence using the subject and the verb on a given line. Write about anything the sentence suggests.

EXAMPLE

handwriting	grumble
anteaters	joust
loneliness	poise

My *handwriting grumbles* onto the page.

Each night, *anteaters joust* with a thousand prey.

Loneliness is *poised* on my doorstep.

Activity 9:
Follow the Leader

The instruction we find in books is like fire. We fetch it from our neighbors, kindle it at home, communicate it to others, and it becomes the property of all.

—Voltaire

It's ironic that there is a great deal about writing that cannot be explained in words, any more than words alone can explain a piece of music. "Follow the Leader" is the writer's version of listening and humming along. For students who have not yet read widely, listening to writing is vital if they are to have any solid idea of what they are trying to do.

Playing follow the leader is very simple. Choose a scene, section, paragraph, or sentence of a published work. Discuss it briefly, read it out loud, and ask students to write their own version following the writer's lead.

We use follow the leader anytime we explain a new writing term or want students to try a particular technique (see "Teacher's Notebook: On Writing Terms," p. 38 and also chapter 4). If we want good characterization, we read a few paragraphs with good characterization; if we want students to try a little dialogue, we start by reading dialogue. If we want to teach a rule of punctuation, we read a sentence, including all the correct punctuation marks, aloud while students copy it. Then, we ask them to write their own sentences following the rule.

Not only is follow the leader a wonderful way to get students started, it is the only method we know to fully explain to students what we want them to try without getting tangled up in windy explanations.

Instructions to Students

Reading and writing go together. The more you read, the easier it is to write; the more you write, the more interested you are in reading. One of the ways to learn about writing is to play "Follow the Leader." Start with a few paragraphs of a story or an article that you like. Read it out loud. Then braindance and downhill to write your own version. Let's try it with a scene from James Herriot's *All Creatures Great and Small* (Bantam, 1978, p. 12). Herriot is one of our favorite authors for follow the leader. Almost any one of his beautifully drawn scenes about everyday life will inspire you to write with depth and imagination.

For those of you who haven't read his books, Herriot is a country veterinarian in the North of England. In this scene he is coming to the door of a clinic in order to interview for a job, and he first meets Mrs. Hall, the housekeeper.

As we read the scene, notice a couple of things. Not very much happens in the scene. Herriot rings the doorbell and Mrs. Hall answers it. That's the whole plot. Notice all the little details: how he describes the door and the dogs. It's the little details that make scenes interesting, not necessarily what happens.

When we finish reading the scene, get out your practice journals. Make up a character and give the character a name. Now make up a house. Write a little scene about what happens to your character at the house. Your version doesn't need to be like Herriot's. It's your own story, except that you should try to use the same kind of details Herriot uses when you tell your story.

EXAMPLES (These examples come from a sixth, seventh, and eighth grade writing workshop. The spelling and paragraphing is the students' own.)

When we got to the porch, I rang the doorbell. Nobody answered. I turned the door-handle and opened the door. We walked in to take a look around. We looked everywhere in the house. There was only one place left, the basement. When we got down to the basement, we saw a crazy looking man, his hair was sticking up, he had a big long nose with a pimple in each nostril, and his clothes were made of trash he found in a garbage can. My friend elbowed me and whispered to me, "He looks like something you'd find in the toilet." He stared at me and then at my friend, then he said he was expecting us. He told us he was a scientist, and he wanted us to test some sort of machine for him. My friend said, "Forget you!" and we both started to run upstairs to escape, but the door shut automatically. We were trapped.

—Mike Sutton, seventh grade

As I was turning, I could see on each side of me emerald green grass, perfectly cut. On the outside of the grass, I could see many beautiful purple and red flowers all standing in a row. When I reached the step, an old cat was lying there, purring softly. When I reached the door, I could see the perfectly cut wood that was carved into the door. As I rang the doorbell, a sound of soothing music floated towards me. When the door finally opened, a beautiful, but older lady came and opened the door. She was the best looking lady I had ever seen. She wore a blue shawl with dark blue pants. Her face was absolutely perfect. She had blue eyes and grayish-white hair. Her nose and mouth were just perfect.

Her house was all white and very clean. She asked me what I wanted. I told her I was collecting paper delivery money.

—Amy Mastran, sixth grade

"Hey! Where is everyone?" I screeched at the top of my voice as I burst into the front door. "Oh great," I thought, "my first day here and my parents want to abandon me."

I walked into the living room. It was still empty, but the dining room furniture was already arranged. There were a few boxes lying around, but I was wondering where all the other furniture was.

I had just walked into the kitchen when I heard a car door slam. Then it was followed by a burst of screaming and shouting from outside. "Well, obviously, dad's home," I sighed.

"Can you believe it! Well, I can't!" he hollered. I was sure the whole neighborhood could hear him.

"What happened?" I asked, hoping he wouldn't have another outburst.

"Would you believe that, because of some mix-up, half of our furniture actually got sent to Egypt! Now some wierdos will be enjoying our furniture while we sleep on the floor tonight!"

Now it was my turn to scream my head off. "Egypt!" I hollered. I stood there in disbelief.

—June Jose, seventh grade

Additional Notes to Teachers

Try to use good published examples. There is little point in asking students to study and follow the example of poor or unedited writing. You don't necessarily need to find samples written at your students' reading level. They can handle surprisingly sophisticated material when it is read to them, and their writing in turn is often equally sophisticated.

If you are using follow the leader to explain a writing term or to demonstrate a writing technique, do the exercise twice using the work of two different writers. Most students will have trouble applying the term or technique in a general way without having modelled at least two different examples.

Follow the leader also provides a good opportunity for a discussion of plagiarism. Follow the leader is not plagiarism. Being inspired by another writer is not the same as copying another's work and calling it one's own. The first is a good way to learn; the second is stealing. Follow the leader is an excellent way to show students the difference.

In *Writing a Novel from Plot to Print*, Lawrence Block points out that the best way to learn outlining is to imitate good outlines, that is, to outline other people's work to see how they put it together.

Try reading a few simple paragraphs out loud while the students copy them down. Read all the punctuation, spell any words the students can't, and tell them when to start a new paragraph. Then discuss the section with the group. (Don't forget to explain that copying for practice is not plagiarism as long as it stays in the practice journal.)

It's worth noting that this is standard practice in the French school system, and French students tend to paragraph beautifully, even though the paragraph is not formally taught. We suspect that routine use of these copied paragraphs may be one of the best ways to teach paragraphing.

Good fiction and poetry examples can be found everywhere. We use a rather eclectic collection, carefully selecting samples from some difficult writers, some genre writers, and some favorite writers. Here's our booklist:

Alice in Wonderland by Lewis Carroll

All Creatures Great and Small and *James Herriot's Dog Stories* by James Herriot

Bridge to Terabithia by Katherine Paterson

Dog Days of Arthur Cane by T. Ernesto Bethancourt

The Dragonriders of Pern by Anne McCaffrey

Fantastic Voyage by Isaac Asimov

A Fine and Pleasant Misery, They Shoot Canoes, Don't They?, and *Never Sniff a Gift Fish* by Patrick McManus

The Gammage Cup by Carol Kendall

Gulag Archipelago by Alexsandr I. Solzhenitsyn

Hangin' Out with Cici by Francine Pascal

The Hobbit by J. R. R. Tolkien

How to Eat Like a Child by Delia Ephron

I, Robot by Isaac Asimov

If I Were in Charge of the World & Other Worries by Judith Viorst (poetry)

Just So Stories by Rudyard Kipling

Lad: A Dog by Albert Payson Terhune

Mr. Tuckett and *Dogsong* by Gary Paulsen

The Racing Game (Odds Against) and *Reflex* by Dick Francis

The Ransom of Red Chief by O. Henry

Rocannon's World by Ursula K. LeGuin

Scary Poems for Rotten Kids by Sean Ohuigin

To Build a Fire by Jack London

The Veldt by Ray Bradbury

Where the Sidewalk Ends: Poems & Drawings by Shel Silverstein

The Wind in the Willows by Kenneth Grahame

Almost anything by Louis L'Amour

We like to use nonfiction examples that are a little closer to our students' reading level, but it doesn't hurt them to hear great nonfiction essayists. Well-written formal nonfiction is very hard to find for younger students. More informal nonfiction is everywhere. We start with the newspaper and popular magazines, most of which are written at the eighth- to ninth-grade reading level. Our favorites are *Popular Science, Omni, Ladies Home Journal, Consumer Reports, National Geographic Inc., Sports Illustrated, The Yankee,* and, of course, *The Writer* and *Writer's Digest Magazine.* Regional magazines often have interesting stories on local history and travel. Check with nearby zoos, aquariums, and museums. Many publish a magazine or newsletter with stories on subjects students can go see for themselves. The same applies to local companies and government. We also like to ask students to bring in their own samples of nonfiction—everything from the instructions on soup cans to their favorite magazines—for a class treasury of good examples.

In order to use more difficult or older works, it's best to explain the background and read the whole piece out loud, then excerpt very small, simple segments. Older students can handle the essay, particularly the informal essays of E. B. White, S. J. Perelman, and James Thurber. *The Bedford Reader*, edited by X. J. Kennedy and Dorothy Kennedy, is an excellent collection of essays organized by technique. Some are good for excerpting for ninth- and tenth-grade students.

More and more science writers are writing popular versions of their technical papers. Our favorite is *The Lives of a Cell: Notes of a Biology Watcher* by Lewis Thomas, but there is an abundance of good science writing for students.

Finally, those magic words "for a transcript, send $2.00" are almost always worth following, particularly if students can see the videotape and compare it to the script.

Teacher's Notebook: More on Giving Assignments

Mixing the craftsman and the artist is extraordinarily easy to do when you give assignments—just tell the students that they are going to write something and spend time talking about how long it should be, whether it should be typed, if spelling counts, etc. Students often drive teachers crazy with questions when writing assignments are given. Answering those questions mixes the artist and the craftsman for the whole assignment.

Planning, polishing, and final production all belong to the craftsman. Drafting and, to some extent, revision belong to the artist. Teach students to separate planning from drafting, drafting from revision, and revision from polishing (see chapter 5) by breaking writing assignments into separate assignments for planning, drafting, revision, and polishing. Refuse to discuss any requirements pertaining to any step of the process other than the current step. Spelling doesn't count until students polish; then it counts.

Teacher's Notebook: On Time in Class for Writing

Always set aside time in class for writing. It's the most important time you spend. Students may not be able to find a good writing environment at home, and they often bog down in complicated questions that their parents can't answer. By the next day, they have forgotten the questions. If students never write in school, many privately conclude that writing isn't very important.

If there isn't time to do all the planning, drafting, and editing in class, set aside a few minutes in class to let students start the assignment. Gathering that first bit of momentum may be the most difficult part of writing. Getting a running start in class makes battling through all the distractions at home a little easier.

Chapter 4

Making It Sound More Adult

CHAPTER CONTENTS

If you're a singer, you lose your voice. A baseball player loses his arm. A writer gets more knowledge, and if he's good, the older he gets the better he writes.

— Micky Spillane

INTRODUCTION

After about age twelve or so, youngsters become very dissatisfied with their writing if it doesn't sound at least a little like the adult writing they read. If they don't learn some technique at this stage, some decide that they can't write. Most rely on advice from older brothers and sisters to try to make their writing sound more grown up. Every teacher knows the homegrown *Student Manual of Style*:

Big-Word-Babble. Use every big word you can remember and make your sentences sound *fancy*. (Some students forget the sentences and just write all the big words they know. All of them forget to say anything. Big word babble is all sound, no meaning.)

Give-'Em-What-They-Like-Syndrome. Just sprinkle in a few words like *however, in conclusion*, and *moreover*. Be sure to include *thus* and *therefore* to keep the teacher happy. (The alternate version is to choose a few good vocabulary words from this week's list or the thesaurus and toss them in at random. Again, saying something is secondary.)

Make-It-Look-Good-Syndrome. Type it up. Throw in some footnotes. Don't run over or under the page limit by so much as a word, even if you must chop off the end to do it. (The alternate version is to pad everything, churning out five pages of useless fluff for every page of clear writing, all saying nothing.)

Copy-the-Encyclopedia-Syndrome. Just copy it out of the encyclopedia to make it sound good. Change a few words here and there to make it your own. (Many students don't even check to see if the borrowed section makes any sense in context. It sounds good, and that's all they want.)

The antidote to these rules is a little solid technical information. Many people don't realize what an enormous fund of technical knowledge even poor adult writers have. The average professional may know as many as 500 more specialized writing techniques than the average adult does. We use the term *technique* loosely. A technique can be almost anything: a rule of punctuation, tips in writing dialogue, a concept (e.g., what's a *scene*, what's a *section*), a writing rule, or suggestions for perking up sentences. Every time students ask "how can I ... ," they want to know a technique. And even sixth-grade students can ask some real stumpers.

This chapter is organized as a mini-dictionary of technical tips for students because technical questions pop up all through the writing process, and unfortunately, answers don't pop to mind so easily. Each entry in the mini-dictionary covers one technique and is divided into two sections: (1) an explanation of the technique, and (2) a list of further tips on the technique called "Tricks of the Trade."

There are thousands of techniques to choose from. We have chosen those that most satisfy the urge to sound more adult. These techniques are not too advanced for seventh and eighth graders. Students gobble up writing techniques that really help them make their writing sound good.

This chapter covers the following techniques: *fiction techniques*—action, description, dialogue, flashback, foreshadowing, introspection, narrative, and scenes; *nonfiction techniques*—anecdote, examples, and sections.

TEACHING THE TECHNIQUES

To convert any technique into a classroom activity, use the explanation together with the follow the leader activity (p. 96) to introduce a technique and ask students to try writing just one scene or section using the technique. Don't ask that students use any particular technique in a complete story. The technique may not apply.

Keep in mind that the distinction between fiction and nonfiction starts to break down at the level of technique. All of the so-called fiction techniques are used routinely in nonfiction, and most of the nonfiction techniques are used occasionally in fiction. We always teach the scene first followed by the fiction techniques. Then we teach the section followed by the nonfiction techniques. Although description, action, and narrative are all used in nonfiction, it is easier for students to learn about them in the context of fiction.

Use the tricks of the trade as handy points for follow-up discussions or as a quick reference when students have editing questions.

One final tip on teaching technique. Cover a range of techniques quickly, rather than covering any one in depth. Slip in a technique here and there among other practice exercises, and keep your presentation quick and light. Beginners usually overdo a new technique. It's a natural part of learning. Knowing a little about a range of techniques helps students more than knowing a great deal about any one.

ACTION

Explanation

Action is what the characters do in a scene, as opposed to *dialogue*, which is what characters say. Action can include big actions (e.g., "Alex jumped from the shed roof to the garden walk and ran to the front of the house") or little actions, sometimes called business (e.g., "Alex set his glass on the counter"). Too much action is hard to follow, so action is almost always woven together with dialogue, introspection, description, or narrative (see later entries).

EXAMPLE

"You will go." *The milk-eyes looked through him to the sea, to the snow, to the line of blue that was the sky.* "You will go now."

And there was such strength in his voice that Russel knew he must go. *He took the handlebar in one hand and pulled the hook, and the dogs surged away and Russel let them run without looking back.*

—Gary Paulsen, *Dogsong*

EXAMPLE

"Hullo," he said, beaming. "Where did you spring from? Come and have a warmer up at the Angel."

I nodded and walked beside him, shuffling on the thawing remains of the previous week's snow.

—Dick Francis, *Flying Finish*

Tricks of the Trade

- Your reader must be able to picture who is coming into and going out of the scene and what the characters are doing. A little bit of business adds color and a sense of a real scene. But readers have good imaginations; you don't need to write down every move your characters make.

- Beginners often try to add zip by adding adverbs: "He walked quickly and quietly from the room." But adverbs slow the action down. If you want to slow it down, fine. If you want to speed it up, use a good strong verb: "He tiptoed from the room." Below is a starter list of strong verbs:

Walked Quickly		Walked Slowly	
dashed	hopped	wandered	dawdled
raced	roared	sauntered	toured
ran	jogged	strolled	traversed
darted	scampered	ambled	hiked
bolted	skittered	rambled	straggled
tore	loped	meandered	limped
jaunted	gallivanted	moseyed	drifted
hastened	scurried	roamed	shuffled
speeded	careened	hobbled	prowled
hurried	skipped	roved	trekked
rushed	fled	crawled	scuttled
escaped	scrambled	staggered	limped
flitted	bounced	toddled	inched
jumped	blasted	wobbled	teetered

- If the strong verbs don't seem strong enough, try an unusual verb. "He whispered away." "She screamed into the driveway."

- *Suddenly.* What to do with all those suddenlies? Because it's an adverb, *suddenly* slows down the action just as it should speed it up. Try crossing it out. Or try to foreshadow it.

EXAMPLE

Change—

Richard spread the newspaper on the dining room table. Suddenly, the tarantula pounced.

to—

Richard flushed away the crumbled tissue and the spider. Big spider, he chuckled. Maria wouldn't know a big spider. Some people were really funny about spiders. Now in Nam, those were big spiders.

He spread the newspaper on the dining room table and settled down to check the stock prices. Not that he owned stocks anymore. It was a habit he couldn't break, something from childhood, like making the bed or cleaning the table after dinner. The day seemed off-color without it. *He glimpsed a furry leg before he saw the tarantula.* Later, all he could remember was two intense spider eyes perched on top of two huge fangs.

ANECDOTES

Explanation

When writers present examples, they sometimes write them as thumbnail stories called *anecdotes*. People like reading stories, even pint-sized stories. Anecdotes written with fiction techniques, such as dialogue or action, are sometimes called *fictional* anecdotes, but the facts of the little story are real. Some short magazine articles are all anecdotes, nothing else.

EXAMPLE

When Rasila decided to buy a dog, she spent several hours debating which set of floppy ears and brown eyes seemed most appealing before a smart pet store owner set her straight. Selecting the breed to match the owner's lifestyle is important, he explained, because personality traits bred into a dog cannot be trained out of it.

Writers become attached to their pens. My favorite word weapon is the cheap cartridge fountain pen. The cheap ones are better than the expensive ones, incidentally. They flow more easily with the ideas. The only problem is replacing them when they gum up. *I spent four hours tracking one down yesterday. I finally found one—just one—buried at the bottom of a rack of designer felt tips and ball points. Ominously, some of the stores no longer carried fountain pens.* If the cheap fountain pen follows the dinosaur into extinction, I may be next.

Tricks of the Trade

- Anecdotes must be short and punchy. Try the three-sentence technique: the first sets up the story, the second contains a crisis, the third leads into the next section with a solution. Television advertisements use this constantly.

EXAMPLE

First sentence setup:	"I could never get grass stains out of the children's clothes."
Second sentence crisis:	"One day, Jimmy's teacher sent him home from school to get a clean shirt."
Third sentence solution:	"Then I discovered Super Sudso Detergent."
Next sentence:	"Yessiree, folks, Super Sudso gets out the toughest stains."

(A word of warning: When you use the three-sentence technique, make sure it doesn't sound like you are selling slicers and dicers for $29.95.)

DESCRIPTION

Explanation

When you tell a story, you want your reader to be able to picture the story. Just writing what your characters say and do isn't enough. "Don't jump!" yelled John. Is John standing on top of a mountain or in a schoolyard? Is John young or old, skinny or fat, tall or short? Remember that reading is more like listening to the radio than watching television. Readers can't imagine what a scene or a character looks like without being told. Use *description* to show the reader what the setting and the characters look like.

EXAMPLE

Tim Archer got into the utility and drove it from the Banbury Feed and General Supply Pty Ltd, down the main street of the town. *The car was a 1946 Chevrolet, somewhat battered by four years of station use, a sturdy practical vehicle with a coupe front seat and an open truck body behind. In this rear portion he was carrying a forty-four gallon drum of Diesel oil, four reels of barbed wire, a can of kerosene, a sack of potatoes, a coil of new sisal rope, a carton of grocieries, and a miscellaneous assortment of spades and jacks and chains that seldom left the truck.*

—Nevil Shute, *A Far Country*

Description often does double duty. It describes and tells the story at the same time. Even though Shute is describing a truck, his reader learns a lot about Tim Archer. He's clearly a farmer, but the word *station* tips us off that the story is set in Australia, and the 1946 Chevrolet lets us know the story takes place after World War II.

Tricks of the Trade

- The trick to writing good description is details. Look how many Shute uses, all of them small. Don't describe everything, just describe a few good details. Use the zoom lens activity (p. 85) to help you choose details.

- Try the *background-middleground-foreground* method of choosing details. Imagine the scene as a picture. Pick a detail on the horizon, a detail in the middle of the picture, and finally, a detail right up close.

EXAMPLE

> *Background*—tractor dust; *middleground*—elm; *foreground*—shovel and tricycle

> The dust from a tractor floated along the horizon, and cicadas sang in the huge elm next to the barn. A battered shovel lay on the lawn next to a shiny new tricycle.

You could also reverse the order, describing the shovel, then the elm, and finally the tractor.

EXAMPLE

> A battered shovel lay on the lawn next to a shiny new tricycle. The cicadas sang in the huge elm next to the barn, and dust from a tractor floated along the horizon.

Adjectives add to description, but too many make it dull. Instead of adding adjectives, use less abstract words. The abstraction ladder helps writers remember the specific words they know. The top rung of the ladder contains the most general words; each rung below that contains more and more specific words. On the bottom rung, write the specific word you've chosen. If you wish, add a short adjective.

EXAMPLE

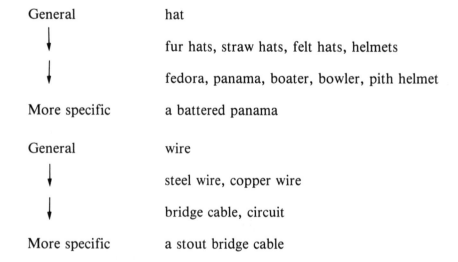

General	hat
More specific	fur hats, straw hats, felt hats, helmets
	fedora, panama, boater, bowler, pith helmet
More specific	a battered panama

General	wire
	steel wire, copper wire
	bridge cable, circuit
More specific	a stout bridge cable

Use a thesaurus, synonym finder, or *What's What* to help you write abstraction ladders.

DIALOGUE

Explanation

Dialogue shows what characters say, just as action shows what they do.

EXAMPLE

Jason dashed through the kitchen, slammed the door behind him and arrived panting in the living room. His sister, Mary, was curled up in the big chair reading a book.

"What do you want?" she asked irritably.

"Oh," Jason replied, glancing over his shoulder, *"nothing really."*

Mary glared at him. *"Don't bug me then."*

"I wasn't. I just ..."

"You were too. You are always bugging me." Mary flounced from the room, leaving Jason with his problem unsolved.

Dialogue sounds as if real people were talking, but it is not written exactly as people talk. That would be dull.

EXAMPLE

"Hi," said Jane.

"Hi," answered Sue.

"Where are you going?" asked Jane.

"English class. I'm not ready for the test."

"Me too."

"I have to go to my locker first."

In dialogue, this conversation is squeezed together and laced with action.

EXAMPLE

Jane caught up with Sue in the hallway. "Hi. Where are you off to in such a hurry?"

"English class," groaned Sue, "and I'm not ready for the test. Better get my notes from my locker."

"You'll be late," warned Jane.

"Tis far, far better to be late than to flunk."

Tricks of the Trade

• Pay some attention to making your dialogue sound like your characters. A cab driver in New York and a cowboy in Arizona do not speak the same way.

• Make sure your reader knows who is speaking. When you write dialogue, start a new paragraph each time a different character speaks. Be sure to say "so-and-so said" if the alternating paragraphs don't make it clear who is speaking.

   Instead of using the word *said*, you can use action to indicate who is speaking. *Said* is usually fine, but you can add emotion or action by using an alternate word for *said*. (Don't overdo it; *said* is best most of the time.) Below is a starter list:

answered	fumed	remarked
asserted	giggled	repeated
babbled	glared	replied
badgered	grieved	responded
bellowed	grinned	retorted
blathered	grumbled	roared
blurted	guessed	screamed
brayed	hollered	shouted
bristled	lamented	sighed
cackled	laughed	snickered
chafed	mimicked	sniggered
chatted	moaned	sniped
chattered	moped	sobbed
cheered	mourned	speculated
chided	murmured	spouted
chortled	nagged	squalled
chuckled	nettled	stewed
claimed	noted	stopped
cried	paused	stormed
croaked	pestered	tittered
crowed	pointed out	wailed
declared	predicted	whined
demanded	promised	whispered
explained	queried	whooped
exploded	raged	worried
fretted	rambled on	yelped

EXAMPLES

Explanation

Examples are the life of the nonfiction party. They make dull ideas come alive. "Not all beautiful trees make good street trees" is pretty ho-hum without examples.

EXAMPLE

Not all beautiful trees make good street trees. *The London plane's iron roots can shred a cement sidewalk or snap a steel water main. Dutch elm disease has nearly wiped out the elm, a popular street tree at the turn of the century. Street trees can't be maintenance headaches or prone to disease. They must grow quickly to a size that can withstand car exhaust and pedestrian vandalism. Their branches should not bat pedestrians in the face or rain sticky sap on parked cars.* That's a lot to ask of a tree.

You can string examples together, or you can use one good example to make your point.

EXAMPLE

Not all beautiful trees make good street trees. *At the turn of the century, elm trees were planted along boulevards and city squares in towns all across the United States. In the 1960s Dutch elm disease—a virus that infects and kills elms—began to spread from east to west stripping city after city of its elegant elms. In the 1980s it picked Denver's boulevards clean and pushed on towards San Francisco.*

Tricks of the Trade

- Deciding how you want to present your example(s) will help you write your section. Think of your examples in three ways: the short example, the extended example, and the story-like example.

    short: "Elms are killed by Dutch elm disease."

    extended: "Elms are killed by Dutch elm disease. By the 1980s, this virus destroyed many of the elms in the United States."

    story-like: see last example of street trees above

- You can use two or three long examples. If, however, you have told a story in the first example that you use, be sure to tell stories of about the same length for the other examples. Otherwise, the later examples will seem incomplete and tacked on.

- Keep the same kinds of examples together. All the examples in the first paragraph illustrate the point, but the examples include specific trees, bad characteristics, and good characteristics. They are presented in groups.

One specialized example is the list. It's used in textbooks and reference books to quickly present a large number of examples in a way that is easy to read.

EXAMPLE

Not all beautiful trees make good street trees. City arborists should not include the following trees on their lists of approved trees:

elms

London planes

large pines with heavy sap

weeping willows

Introduce examples with *for example* or *such as* if it might not be clear to your reader that you are giving an example.

EXAMPLES

Not all beautiful trees make good street trees. The elm, for example, is gorgeous, but a poor choice for a street tree.

Trees such as the elm, the London plane, and the weeping willow should not be used for street tree plantings.

FLASHBACK

Explanation

Writers don't like to begin at the beginning. They like to start stories or chapters with a high point, not background. After they have the reader's attention, they use *flashback* to fill in the background from an earlier time.

EXAMPLE

Jim Baker swore Dannie would never drag him out for another vacation. He urged the ancient horse along, but it was determined to storm the mountain one aching step at a time.

"Isn't this fun?" laughed Dannie. She guided her elderly mare alongside Jim's horse.

"Great fun for an interior decorator from Manhattan maybe," thought Jim. *He remembered the time his best friend Bob had signed them both up to ride the broncs in the Alamosa Days Rodeo. They were both just kids, but Bob's dad was a rancher and put a high price on horsemanship ...*

Tricks of the Trade

- Flashback is a useful tool, but getting into and out of a flashback can be a bit tricky. Most stories are written in past tense, so the first sentence of the flashback must use *had* (had signed, had gone, had flown, had begun, etc.). It's best to use *remembered, recalled, thought back,* or *reminisced about the time* to introduce the flashback.

  The easiest way to get out of the flashback and back to the story is to have a character from the present scene, such as Dannie, say something. ("Oh look! A deer!" cried Dannie.) Action also works. (Jim's horse halted abruptly.) Avoid introspection, description, or narrative. They can be used, but it's easy to confuse your reader.

FORESHADOWING

Explanation

Sometimes you need to hint at something that is going to happen later in the story—to *foreshadow* what will happen.

Foreshadowing builds suspense. It also helps you plant clues in mysteries, provide future escapes for trapped adventures, and other handy necessities. In the nineteenth century, writers would foreshadow with sentences such as "little did she know that buying an apple could ruin her life forever." Today such foreshadowing is thought heavy-handed, but the idea is the same.

Suppose you are planning later in your story to trap your hero in the bedroom of an old house. Most bedrooms have windows. Why doesn't your hero escape through the window? You could say there are no windows, and your reader would reply, "how terribly convenient for the writer." Try foreshadowing a reason why the window won't work. For example, early in the story, a character can wash the window and comment on what a long way it is to the ground from that bedroom window. You can make the window into a French door and have a character accidentally drop the key to the door down a heating vent. Your imagination is the only limit.

You can also plant clues in mysteries with foreshadowing. In your story, if Detective Snoop desperately searches the mug books all morning, then just happens to pick up the criminal's wallet on the street while he's on his way to the coffee shop, the coincidence is too convenient. But suppose back in the beginning of the story, Detective Snoop's neighbor drops by to return some sugar, hands him a wallet that she found on the bus, and asks him to take it to the lost and found. Snoop throws it in his glove compartment and forgets it. Then, when he's desperately searching the mug books, he can remember the wallet when he sees a familiar face. Much better.

Tricks of the Trade

- Remember, you don't need to write the story in order. If you find that you need some foreshadowing earlier in the story, go back and insert it at the appropriate point.

INTROSPECTION

Explanation

Introspection shows the reader what your characters think. You can present the thoughts of characters using either *introspection* or *internal dialogue*.

EXAMPLE

Introspection:

Allen raced to the bus stop. *He couldn't be late again. It was the third time—and that could only mean detention. Mom wasn't going to understand ...*

Internal dialogue:

Allen raced to the bus stop. *Oh no, he thought. I can't be late again. It's my third time. I'll get detention. I don't think Mom's going to understand ...*

Tricks of the Trade

- To save your reader confusion, stick with the point of view of one character all through the scene. Don't switch from the thoughts of one character to the thoughts of another.

- To move out of introspection and back into the scene, use the flashback reentry technique: interrupt the character's thoughts with dialogue or action from the scene.

NARRATIVE

Explanation

Narrative tells the story, whereas dialogue, action, introspection, and description *show* the story. In nonfiction, narrative also tells about the idea, whereas examples, anecdotes, and description show the idea.

Narrative is essential. Even "Show, Don't Tell" can be overdone, and narrative moves the story along. Nothing, however, is duller than long paragraphs of narrative, even well-written narrative. Use narrative for a purpose, keep it brief, and practice writing richer narrative.

Beginners often write their first stories entirely in narrative:

EXAMPLE

Then Bill decided to leave India, so he got on a train and went to Nepal. In Kathmandu he met a man in a white suit. Bill thought the man was bad, so he called his boss in America and asked him what to do. Then ...

or

> Fort Sumter is in Charleston Harbor, South Carolina. It's important because the first shots in the Civil War were fired there in 1861.

There is nothing wrong with a good simple narrative sentence, but consider making it into a scene. If it's not important enough to become a scene, try enriching the narrative with a little description, action, or dialogue. First write a few simple narrative sentences, but don't use *go* or *went*. Be specific about what happened:

EXAMPLE

> Bill got on the train at the Calcutta station. Four days later, he arrived in Nepal. When he got off the train, he was greeted by a man in a white suit.

Once you have done this, rewrite these sentences enriching them with more detail.

EXAMPLE

> When Bill finally climbed the steps to the Calcutta train station, the platform was packed with a thousand people, shouting and pushing. They shoved battered suitcases and curious parcels into one another's backs as they fought to reach seats close to the open windows but far from the locomotive's engines. After a twenty-minute struggle, he finally wedged himself into an aisle seat near the center of the train. Four days later, he stepped off an elderly bus onto the streets of Kathmandu. With his first breath of cool mountain air, all thought of steamy, crowded Calcutta slipped away.
> "Welcome, Mr. Mendal," said a voice behind him.
> Bill turned. The speaker was an odd little man in an impeccable white suit.

You can also enrich nonfiction narrative, although you needn't get carried away. Enrich it with a few more facts, a little description, a tiny anecdote.

EXAMPLE

> The city of Charleston, S.C., is a city of azaleas and graceful colonial homes. Before the Civil War, its busy harbor was the major Southern port for shipping tobacco and textiles to the wealthy in England and the home of Fort Sumter. Believing that Fort Sumter gave the North a bird's-eye view of one of the South's most precious trade links, Southern Confederates surrounded the Fort on April 2, 1861 and ordered its commander to surrender. When he refused, they fired on the fort, and the Civil War began.

Tricks of the Trade

• Use your encyclopedia and a good atlas to learn details. Moving a character from one exotic place to another is a wonderful way to learn about world geography and map reading. Because narrative moves so quickly, it requires more research than other parts of the story.

For the passage about Calcutta above, we used an atlas to discover, for example, that there is no train from Calcutta to Nepal. The train stops at Monghyr, about 200 miles from Kathmandu, the capital of Nepal, and the trip would have to be finished by bus. Using our compass, we measured about 700 miles by train and road from Calcutta to Kathmandu. With delays or irregular bus service, we guessed that might take four days. Kathmandu (population 395,000) is the only place in Nepal large enough to be likely to have regular bus service. From our desk encyclopedia, we learned that Calcutta is the oldest, most overcrowded city in India (9,000,000 people). It is extremely hot and humid by contrast to Kathmandu, which is in a high mountain valley, with temperatures often below freezing.

We could have gone further and found out for sure if the train from Calcutta to Monghyr was diesel or steam, what the passenger cars look like, exactly how long such a trip might take, etc. We might have tried to discover what the weather would be like in both cities during a certain month of the year.

The need for realistic facts to write the story makes pursuing the facts a pleasure. Conduct a little treasure hunt. Use your imagination for research. It's a fun way to learn. Writing a paragraph about steamy, crowded Calcutta and crisp, cool Kathmandu will make your geography memorable for many years. You may never forget that there is no train from Calcutta to Kathmandu.

Research can also enrich nonfiction. There are whole books written about Charleston and Fort Sumter, but an encyclopedia and other reference books can help you find just a few extra details to draw a better picture of graceful Charleston and to depict the opening shot of the war. Use the facts to help you enrich your writing; don't copy them.

- Use words such as *told*, *explained*, *went*, and *left* in narration to cut out repetitive dialogue or action.

EXAMPLES

Mary told Priscilla about the ghost.

Mike went to the store. He wasn't gone long, but when he got home ...

- Somewhere along the line, someone is going to tell you never to use *I* or *we* in nonfiction. This is not necessarily good advice. Some types of nonfiction, such as personal experiences, need *I* or *we*. What is meant is to avoid intruding on your narrative with "I think" or "we believe." Just tell the story. The whole piece is what you think; you don't need to say it. The trick to writing warm, friendly nonfiction is to go ahead and write your draft using *I* or, if you are coauthoring, *we*. Then go back and cut any *I* or *we* that you don't need. If you are not coauthoring, don't use *we* at all. You'll sound like an old-fashioned nurse: "We must take our medicine now, mustn't we?"

RULES ON "WRITING RULES"

Explanation

Every writing technique, from scene construction to punctuation, has an accompanying set of rules. While these guides are a big help to experienced writers, they often cause more harm than good to beginners.

Professionals don't treat writing rules the same way that novices do. Professionals look on them as ideas to be tested, not laws to be obeyed. Knowing what good writing is, they will cheerfully break a rule to improve the writing and happily attack any copyeditor who tries to change the decision. They also have enough experience to know the full rule, not an oversimplified version of it. For example, students are often told: "Don't repeat words." The full rule is: "Vary your words within reason, but deliberately repeat key words for transition, emphasis, and unity"—a very different rule. Working writers also know which rules take priority over others, something students do not.

Because writing rules are so pervasive and so often misused, a few rules on rules may help students:

1. Go easy on the rules. The secret to good writing is not to overdo anything, including the rules. Treat rules as rules of thumb. Always prefer good writing to following a rule.

2. Use your judgment. Remember, nobody knows all the rules—not your teachers, not your older sister or brother, not your parents, not even Shakespeare. Don't follow rules because other people suggest it unless you feel it improves the result.

3. Some rules are more important than others. They should always come first:

    *   *Be clear.* If your reader can't understand you, nothing else makes a bit of difference.

    *   *Enjoy your own work.* If you would not want to read it, why should other people?

    *   *Care about your reader.* How lucky you are that another person has taken the time to read what you wrote. Take care of your reader. Make it easy to read, and put your whole self into it. Write with enthusiasm. Make it something special.

    *   *Be honest.* Don't pad, don't plagiarize, and don't try to sound fancy. Give your own point of view in your own words.

    *   *Make up your own rules.* If you find something that helps you write, record it in your personal journal. Your own rules are the most important rules. They are especially designed to help *you.*

SCENES

Explanation

One of the things that will help your writing sound more adult is to practice writing one scene at a time. A *scene* is just a small section of the story. Think of it as a little story within your bigger story.

There are two ways you can present the story. You could write a simple sentence telling the plot: "John went to the old house where he met a man who told him about a buried treasure." (Don't let the word *plot* worry you. As Paul Darcy Boles says in *Story-crafting*, "all Plot has ever meant is *What happens first* and then *What happens next.*")

The little sentences of plot tell the story, but a whole story told this way becomes a boring list of what happened first, then what happened next. You could also write this part of the plot as a scene. A scene doesn't just tell the story, it *shows* the story.

EXAMPLE

The house was easy enough to find. It was an ancient Victorian sitting in the middle of a spanking new suburban development. Huge trees and a weedy gravel driveway marked it as the farmhouse that once presided over the fields now turned into tidy lawns and matching driveways. A television blared from behind the screen door.

"Mr. Hatford?" asked John through the screen.

"Go away!" shouted a voice.

"Maureen sent me. She couldn't get off work. You said it was urgent."

The sound of the game show snapped off, and an elderly man shuffled to the door.

"Who are you?" Hatford hooked the door closed.

"A friend of Maureen's."

"A lawyer?"

"No."

"One of them banker boyfriends of hers?"

John grinned. "No. Actually, I ... I guess you could say I'm unemployed."

"Oh well, that's okay then," Hatford unlatched the door and motioned John in. "I keep telling Maureen that we gotta be careful. She's just too trusting, that girl. One of these days, she'll have trouble."

To write a scene, the writer weaves description, dialogue, action, introspection, and narrative together like threads in a braid. These are sometimes called the *fiction tools*, although they are often used in nonfiction as well. Here's a list of these tools:

Description: describes the setting or the characters

Dialogue: what the characters say

Action: what the characters do

Introspection: what the characters think

Narrative: what happened in a simple sentence (telling the story instead of showing it)

See our other mini-dictionary entries for more detail on each of these.

Tricks of the Trade

- Not every part of the story is told in scenes, just the most important parts. The next time you are reading a story or a novel, see if you can pick out the scenes. When you are choosing which parts of your own story to write as scenes, start with important scenes that move the story forward.

- Don't pack too much plot into a scene. Most scenes take place in one setting with a certain set of characters. If too much happens, the scene becomes too long. It sometimes helps to write the scene as one or two narrative sentences, like we did with John and Mr. Hatford, before you rewrite it as a scene.

• Remember that scenes are little stories within stories. Each scene has a high point somewhere in it. It may not be very exciting, but it's a little more exciting than the other parts of the scene.

SECTIONS

Explanation

A *section* in nonfiction is just like a scene in fiction, but instead of showing a reader a small piece of the plot, the section takes a simple idea and shows it to the reader with examples, anecdotes, description, and narrative. Here's an example from an essay in *The Lives of a Cell* by Lewis Thomas. The simple idea is that "ant colonies act like people."

EXAMPLE

> Ants are so much like human beings as to be an embarrassment. They farm fungi, raise aphids as livestock, launch armies into wars, use chemical sprays to alarm and confuse enemies, capture slaves. The families of weaver ants engage in child labor, holding their larvae like shuttles to spin out the thread that sews the leaves together for their fungus gardens. They exchange information ceaselessly. They do everything but watch television.

Thomas doesn't just *tell* us that ants are like people. He *shows* us six different things ants do that human civilizations have also done: farming, raising livestock, fighting, employing slavery and child labor, and exchanging information.

A nonfiction section doesn't just show examples—it has a pattern or a plan. The ant examples are presented in the order of the growth of human civilization, from farming to television.

Do you think Thomas got his section all organized on the first draft? Probably not. More likely, he write down six ways ants act like people in his first draft. Then he decided to organize those six ways by the order of the rise of human civilizations. He may have had to find out whether farming or herding came first. He might have had to throw out an example that didn't fit the plan, then find another example of ant behavior to fit the plan. Then he rewrote the whole thing. This is how writing nonfiction often works.

Writing a nonfiction section is a lot like cleaning out a closet. First, you must take out all the junk. (You call it *research*, but it is really just a bunch of ideas, examples, facts, descriptions, and so forth—junk until you do something with it.) Once you've piled everything up, you decide which particular junk you want to put in this particular closet and get rid of the junk you don't want. *Then* you put everything away in the closet following a plan. It looks wonderful once you've finished, but getting it done is messy.

Because writing nonfiction is always messy, it is a good idea to plan on writing three trial drafts:

First trial— choose your simple idea and get the interesting details down

Second trial— organize it into a little plan:
- throw out details that don't fit
- organize those you save
- add more details if necessary

Third trial— rewrite it in order to tidy everything up and smooth it out

The nonfiction writer writes each section weaving together examples, anecdotes, description, and narrative, much like the fiction writer weaves dialogue and action together to make a scene. But the nonfiction writer does not use quite so many different tools; normally, nonfiction writers combine narrative with one other tool. Thomas uses only examples and one narrative sentence: "Ants are so much like people as to be an embarrassment."

All the fiction tools are also used in nonfiction. Sections of some types of nonfiction, such as personal experience stories, are written like fiction scenes, but you won't find much dialogue, action, or instrospection in other types of nonfiction. Below are the tools most often used in nonfiction:

Example: a specific instance of something

Anecdote: a thumbnail story illustrating a point

Description: describes people, places, or things

Narrative: tells the story, explains the point, or gives reasons

See our other mini-dictionary entries for more detail.

Tricks of the Trade

- Information makes nonfiction interesting. Notice how much information about ant behavior Thomas packs into one small paragraph. If you are having trouble with a nonfiction section, go get more information. Read more books; look up more facts; make yourself into an expert. The better you know your subject, the easier it is to write nonfiction.

Chapter 5

Editing with Enthusiasm

CHAPTER CONTENTS

*An editor should tell the writer his work is better
than it is; not a lot better, a little better.*
—T. S. Eliot

INTRODUCTION

Editing is an acquired taste, right up there with oysters and fried squid. Students won't undertake it naturally, but with a proper introduction, there is no reason they can't enjoy it. After all, the perfect first draft is an awful burden. It kills creativity with premature judgment and makes drafting harder by mixing the artist and the craftsman. A proper introduction to editing is the key to persuading students to try it, however. Approach is nine-tenths of the problem.

Some schools using the writing process have called editing "getting it right." This may be a poor choice of words. Editing is not simply a matter of correcting errors—it's much more. Creativity is a process of creating something, then adjusting it. Those adjustments include changes to meet the writer's creative expectations as well as corrections of mechanical errors. When students revise their work to match their own aesthetic sense, they gain a tremendous sense of power. Rather than feeling helpless when they do not succeed on the first attempt, they feel in charge of their writing and more responsible for it. Once they feel in charge, they take more pride in the results. Building confidence and taking pride, not "getting it right," are the real reasons for teaching students to edit.

Separating Revision and Polishing

There are two phases to editing: revision and polishing. Students must first learn to separate them and then learn to finish revising before they start to polish. Mixing revision with polishing invariably creates not only more work but many other problems as well.

Revision includes improving clarity, structure, and readability. Students learn to adjust their writing to match their own creative expectations when they revise. Revision is also writing based. That is, students can discuss revisions using the same terminology and decide on changes using what they know about planning, drafting, or technique. Revision and drafting are so intimately connected that, for some writers, writing *is* revision. From the writer's point of view, revision is the most important phase of editing. But it's not a question of getting it right. There is not any right way to revise a piece any more than there is any right way to write it. It's a matter of reworking the piece until the writer feels satisfied.

Polishing includes checking the sentence structure and the finer points of style, improving the punctuation, correcting spelling errors, and finally producing attractive copy. Unlike revision, polishing is not writing based. Each area of polishing is based on an underlying set of skills completely unconnected with the rest of the writing process. For example, a person can know the rules of punctuation backwards and forwards and still write badly. The reverse is also true. Many talented writers will cheerfully admit that their punctuation is shaky, even though they write well and publish often.

This is a confusing point, so be very careful about it. Writing is a confidence game. The tentative or uncertain writer always has trouble. Students are not very confident about their underlying style, spelling, punctuation, and even handwriting skills. If they confuse good spelling, punctuation, or presentation with good *writing*, they may lose confidence in their writing. Some conclude that they can't write because they can't spell. Others avoid putting in any punctuation at all. Still others lose confidence in their ideas and try to cover them up with unreadable handwriting. To avoid these problems, teach the skills underlying polishing in separate lessons, separate revision and polishing, and use a very light touch with polishing.

Polishing the physical appearance of a piece is the last step to polishing and worth special mention. Polishing the presentation can include anything from making a neat handwritten copy to a full-scale printing. It does not have anything to do with writing per se. Good penmanship or typing skills may help a student get the words on the page less painfully, but they are not requirements. A messy but well written story is still well written.

On the other hand, the world may permit F. Scott Fitzgerald to send in manuscripts scribbled on the back of envelopes. It is less tolerant of the rest of us. An attractive presentation can make the difference between a sale and a rejection slip for a professional writer, and teachers rarely give students full credit for good writing if the presentation is a mess. Because students are always surprised by the amount of time editing consumes, they tend to run out of time and give presentation short shrift. Students should learn to present their work attractively, and they will learn to do a better job if you consistently make sure they finish all the other phases of editing and then give them extra time to work on their presentation.

Selecting Pieces for Editing

Planning and drafting is slow work, but editing is glacial. If students allow twice as much time for editing as drafting, they won't be far off the mark. Because there simply isn't time in the school year for students to thoroughly edit every piece they write, teachers need to decide what degree of editing they can reasonably expect.

We prefer to let students choose a few pieces each term to take all the way through the process rather than asking them to do minor editing on every piece of work. Students who choose which pieces to edit have more stake in the results. Each time they thoroughly edit a piece, they learn what it really takes to finish a piece of writing.

Recopying a rough draft so that an editor can read it is often the only editing students need do. However, these pieces should be always be clearly labeled as "neatly recopied rough drafts" or "neat first drafts" so that students do not confuse partially complete work with finished work.

Distinguishing Editing from Criticism

Before you can get anywhere with students, you must also distinguish between editing and criticism. People can be surprisingly cruel about writing. Even sixth and seventh grade students may have received painful criticism of their writing and are leery of the idea of editing because of the experience. The job of the editor and that of the critic only appear to be similar. There is a big difference—a difference too often overlooked.

No sane student—no sane person—shares a rough draft in order to be shot to pieces. When writers begin to edit, they are *still* writing and have a long way to go before they finish. They are already exhausted and need encouragement to carry on, or they will never finish. Writers do not need criticism at this stage. Those who give it are showing their ignorance.

Writers do need a friendly ear, a fresh pair of eyes, and a different point of view to help them find places that need improvement. They also need a sharp mind to suggest possible changes. Finally, they need a pat on the back to boost their flagging energy. The person who provides all these things is the editor. Good writers love good editors because they are the writer's biggest help and best friends.

On the other hand, criticism can be devastating to writers. T. S. Eliot moved to England and could not write for a year and a half after a heavy bout with some critics. It damages students to encourage them to throw their hearts into writing something if they are not also protected from the fickle opinions of critics. No writer should judge his or her own work on the opinion of one or two other people.

We tell our students that once a piece is finished, anybody has a right to comment. These are critics. They can say whatever they want for whatever reason. Some critics are serious; others are just showing off at the expense of the writer; some are thoughtful; some just silly. Whereas students should listen to suggestions from a good editor, they have every right to ignore a critic. The writer did not ask for the critic's opinion and does not need to listen—even if the critic is a teacher.

Establishing a System

Editing can be complicated and confusing. You need to pull it together into a simple editing system that is predictable, positive, and based on editing to publish. It doesn't matter what the particular system is as long as it meets these criteria.

Some teachers prefer to serve as editor, but we think the teacher has too much authority to do it well. Teachers' comments, both positive and negative, cut too deep. We prefer a system where students edit each other's work while the teacher serves as publisher, providing technical assistance and giving final approval. We also include the grading system in the editing system in order to insure that the two are compatible.

A Simple System

The Editing Process. Break editing into a two-step process: revision and polishing. Break polishing into a series of smaller steps: style, punctuation and spelling, and presentation. Teach students to take each step one at a time and to seek the approval of the writing group before moving from one step to the next.

The Publishing Payoff. Define *published* works as finished pieces students share outside of their writing group. Publish in some small way every piece a student takes all the way through the editing process. For example, display published pieces on the "Authors of the Week" bulletin board or hold readings in class on a regular basis. Store all published pieces in the student's portfolio.

Authors. Authors are responsible for choosing which pieces to edit and for making the final decision on every suggestion.

Editors. The writing group is responsible for editing the work of every student in the group. Unless the writing group requests it, the teacher will not read the work until it has been through the group several times.

The Publisher. The teacher serves as *publisher* most of the time. The publisher is responsible for providing technical assistance to the writing groups and helping students find ways to publish. No piece is published without the publisher's approval.

Grades. Grades are based on doing a certain number of practice pieces, publishing a certain number of pieces, and serving as editor and copyeditor for at least one other student during the school term. Students know in advance what they need to do to achieve a particular grade.

In this system the payoff for writing and careful editing is not a grade or, indeed, the opinion of any one person; it is getting published. Every student who finishes a piece and achieves the portfolio gets special attention and can take pride in the accomplishment. At the same time the teacher can exercise quality control by refusing to publish unfinished or inadequate work. Students work with a predictable set of editors who must also share their work with the group. The grading system is also very predictable. For practical purposes, students can choose the grade they wish to achieve and work toward the goal.

In this chapter we've collected explanations of editing which we think help students get started, along with a series of handouts we use to explain each editing step. The activities in the first part define editing and the roles of *editors* and *authors*. Activity 3 introduces students to the *revision loop*, a simple method for identifying what to revise and for generating editorial suggestions. The second part of this chapter has a series of polishing handouts we use to introduce students to the basics without swamping them in a thousand rules and requirements.

INTRODUCING EDITING

Let's be honest. The best way to learn to edit is to follow a good example. In the best of all possible worlds, beginning writers would take several manuscripts all the way through the editing process under the guidance of an experienced editor. So much for pipe dreams. Even if all teachers were skilled editors, one person cannot possibly do editorial justice to a hundred or more students a day. The next best option to one-on-one editing with a seasoned editor is to have students edit each other's work. They do a surprisingly good job if they have clearly defined roles and a process to follow. We use the activities in this section to get students started by explaining what editing is, defining the roles of editors and authors, and giving them a simple process for revision.

One note of warning. Editing is one of the last great crafts in an age of mass production. Like all crafts, it takes time to develop any skill at all. Do not expect students to automatically improve their work through editing. Beginning editors stand a good chance of ruining a draft. When students wreck a piece with their first editorial efforts—and they will—you can try to persuade them to start again with the original draft, but they probably won't agree. There is nothing you can do about this. Cringe and accept their decision. It's part of learning.

Activity 1:
Editing? What's Editing?

Few processes are more wonderful ... than that of making your manuscript shine where it was rusty, tighten where it was flabby, speak clearly where it mumbled.

      —Paul Darcy Boles

We use this little explanation and handout to introduce students to editing.

Instructions to Students

What is editing exactly? Writing a story or an article is a little like creating a garden. The gardener plans the garden by imagining what the garden should look like, deciding where to put the corn and the radishes, and choosing the seeds—very much like a writer plans the piece. Whereas the gardener prepares the soil, plants the seeds, and waters the garden, the writer drafts. But the job is not finished. The gardener has weeds to pull, dead plants to remove, and pretty new plants to add before the garden looks its best. So does the writer. There are weedy words to pull, unclear sentences to straighten out, sections that need to be rearranged—all to make the writing its shining best. That's editing.

There are two steps to editing:

STEP 1.   Revision.

You want to make sure your piece is easy to understand and fun to read first. To do this, you revise. When you revise, you can cut out some words, sentences, or paragraphs. You can add others. Sometimes, you will need to rearrange paragraphs or sentences and to rewrite others. Revision is always the first step to editing. It's always exciting because you can shape what you said to sound just like you wish without worrying about deciding what to say, as you did when you drafted the piece.

STEP 2.   Polishing.

Polishing puts the final gloss on your work. When you polish, you check the style, spelling, and punctuation. You also change any little thing that you feel would smooth out the writing. The last step of polishing is typing or neatly recopying the piece so that it looks attractive and is easy to read.

Technically, polishing your presentation is the last step to editing, but there really is one more step.

STEP 3.   Publishing.

Why go to all that work if you don't share your story with readers? Any time you share your finished work outside of your writing group, you have published it. Publishing is the reason for revising and polishing your stories. You edit because you want to share, to publish.

The person in charge of publishing an author's work is called the *publisher*. The publisher in this class is the teacher. The publisher helps authors and editors solve any problems they can't figure out, gives the final approval for publishing, and helps the author find ways to publish.

We're going to tell you more about revision, polishing, production, and publishing as you do it, but in the meantime, we have some rules that apply to all the steps of editing. We call them the Golden Rules of Editing.

THE GOLDEN RULES OF EDITING (HANDOUT)

Rule #1:   When in doubt, read out loud.

The most important part of editing is reading the work out loud to be sure that it sounds just like the author wants it to sound. If you have a question, read the whole piece, the paragraph, or the sentence out loud. Does it sound right? If it sounds right, it probably is.

Rule #2:   Take your time.

Editing takes time, but it is time well spent because editing takes your good work and makes it the best it can be. If you are tired, wait a little before starting back to work. Editing at a steady pace with small breaks always works better than a crash project.

Rule #3:   Don't mix revision and polishing.

Finish revising before you start to polish. Mixing revision and polishing always makes a mess. Also, finish each step of the polishing before you begin the next. Editing is always easier if you work on one thing at a time.

Rule #4:   Always work from big to little.

Start with big changes, such as moving whole sections or scenes around. Work back to little things, such as changing a word in a sentence. It makes no sense to revise a sentence if you cut it out five minutes later when you move a whole section around.

Rule #5:   Finish.

If you don't finish, how well you write or the care you take to polish won't matter a bit. Nobody can read it until it's done. You can take little pauses to refresh your energy, but otherwise just do the best job you can and keep going until you finish.

Activity 2:
The Editor? Who's That?

No passion in the world is equal to
the passion to alter someone else's draft.
—H. G. Wells

Good editors are about as rare as large diamonds; the rest of the world muddles along with a confused idea of the job. Reading rough drafts to strangers is a frightening, unpredictable process. Keep student editing groups together for the whole term. Because students have so few good role models—and so many bad ones—start them off with a careful explanation of both the role of the editor and the proper attitude toward editing. We use this little explanation and handout.

Instructions to Students

When you edit your work, your attitude is very important. Remember the artist and the craftsman? (See chapter 3.) Well, the artist is in charge of drafting, but the craftsman is in charge of editing. The artist is enthusiastic, emotional, involved, and sensitive. The craftsman, on the other hand, is more like Dr. Spock in the *Star Trek* movies. Dr. Spock is concerned, but he's also detached and logical. While everyone else runs around yelling, Spock stays cool. He listens and comes up with good ideas to solve the problem. He's also patient and takes things one step at a time.

Notice that the attitude of the craftsman is almost the opposite of that of the artist. When editing your work, first tell your artist to take a vacation. Then tell your craftsman to get busy.

The Job of the Editor

You must draft alone, but you don't need to edit alone. You can get help from someone else's craftsman. This outside helper is called an *editor*. The editor can be a fellow student, a friend, or a teacher.

What an editor really does is give the author a fresh pair of eyes and another viewpoint on the work. A good editor is the author's best friend. When the author is tired, the editor is sympathetic and helps out. When the author knows something doesn't work, the editor tries to figure out what needs changing. When the author can't find an error, such as a spelling mistake, the editor tries to spot it. When the author can't think of ideas, the editor comes up with suggestions. Any time the author's artist pops up with silly emotions, the editor says, "Be logical. Cool down," and gets the author back on track. In our class the members of your writing group will also serve as editors for one another.

The author's craftsman and the editor's craftsman work together. On editing days, sometimes you will be an author and sometimes you will be an editor for another student. This works well, as long as authors and editors all remember that both are really craftsmen working together. We don't want to be negative, but we must warn you that when either authors or editors do not act like calm, detached craftsmen, the group will have trouble.

When authors act like artists

- they won't listen

- they argue over everything

- they get upset

- they take every comment as a criticism

- they tire out and don't want to finish

- they are impatient

When editors are bad craftsmen

- they criticize without helping

- they don't take their job seriously

- they make fun of the author or show off at the author's expense

- they aren't specific

- they don't make helpful suggestions

If the members of your writing group work together as craftsmen, you'll be dynamite. You can help each other so much that you won't believe it. We want everyone in our class to learn to be good editors, so we have a handout to remind you of some things each of you should do to be good editors.

GOOD EDITORS (HANDOUT)

1. Good editors are good craftsmen. They learn as much as they can about writing and apply what they know in a detailed, careful way.

2. Good editors are specific. They don't say, "That's dumb," or "I like that." They say, "Your high point needs more suspense," or "The description in this scene is really good."

3. Good editors don't boss. It's the author's piece, not the editor's. The good editor makes good suggestions and leaves decisions to the author.

4. Good editors help the author finish. They give the author some pats on the back and say, "Keep going. You're almost finished, and I know you can do it."

5. Good editors help the author take things one step at a time until it's all done.

6. Good editors take the job seriously. They feel as proud of the finished piece as the author does. And well they should.

Activity 3:
The Revision Loop

*What is true of friendship is true of editing; ... I have tried to
remember that it was my job to help when the author needed
it, to reassure him, to call out of him his best, but always to
bear in mind that the final decision was his.*

— Edward Weeks

For some people, the first draft holds no thrills; only upon revising do they really begin to write.
Their motto is, "Just give me a telephone directory, anything but a blank page. I'll revise it into
something." In every group of students, you will discover a few who catch fire once they discover
revision.

The "Revision Loop" gives students a simple, positive procedure to follow in order to identify
portions of the draft that need revision and to decide how to go about changing them. Before students
begin to use the loop, make sure that they feel comfortable with the idea of sharing their work by
giving them practice reading aloud without comment.

Instructions to Students

Up until now, you have been sharing your work with the other people in your writing group.
Today, each of you is going to revise your piece with the help of your writing group.

The word *revise* means to *see again*. When you draft, you get your story out on paper where you
can see it, but no writer finishes on the first draft. It's too hard to think of things to say, write them
out, get them organized, and make sure that your work is clear and easy to read all at once. There are
too many different things going on. You need to set your piece aside for a little while, then take
another look. When you see it again, you will find all sorts of things you missed while you were
drafting. Some of those things will be good — better than you realized. Other parts will need a little
more work to sound just right.

Revision is the writer's secret weapon. When musicians hit a sour note or downhill skiers take a
spill, they can only try to do better the next time. The writer, on the other hand, can revise.

A reader may think that a piece turned out perfectly the first time, but the writer knows better.
Good writers revise and revise and revise until they are satisfied that their work sounds just right. Did
you know that Ernest Hemingway revised the end of *A Farewell to Arms* thirty-nine times? Most
professionals revise everything at least four or five times. That's why their writing sounds so good.

Of course, you don't need to revise everything thirty-nine times, but you should learn to revise
your work until you are satisfied that it sounds right. One of the things that will help you and your
editors revise is the "Revision Loop."

(Text continues on page 136.)

THE REVISION LOOP (HANDOUT)

1.   Group chooses an editorial question.

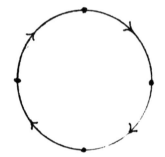

4.   The author revises.

2.   Author reads piece
     to group.

3.   Editors make editorial suggestions.

STEP 1.   The group starts around the loop by choosing an editorial question.

Editorial questions can be about almost anything: "What is the best part?" "How can the author make the dialogue fit the characters better?" "Which sections are not clear?" "How can the author make the end more satisfying?" "How should the author add suspense?" (See the Basic Editorial Questions handout [p. 134] for ideas on questions to ask.)

Choosing those editorial questions which will most help the author is the trick to revising. You can go around the loop as many times as you wish, but there are a thousand possible editorial questions. Editors and authors should go around on at least the three or four questions that they think will most help the author.

The group can choose any questions they wish except for the first question. The first editorial question is always "What is the best part?" Strangely, authors do not know which parts of their own stories are best. If their editors forget to mention which parts are best, the authors may accidentally throw them out when they revise.

STEP 2.   Next, the author reads the piece aloud while the editor(s) listen carefully keeping the editorial question in mind.

Reading aloud is the most important part of editing. Revision may be a bad word because authors and editors do not need to see a piece; they need to *hear* it. (Remember, writing is like singing. Until a piece is read aloud, it is like an unsung song.) While the author reads, the editors listen carefully with the editorial question in mind and make notes.

One detail that you should know is that the first time the author reads a draft out loud, some little things called *klunkers* will probably show up. A klunker is no big deal. It's just a place where the writer's imagination moved faster than his pen. The result is missing words or scrambled sentences. Everybody—including the author—says, "huh?" Fix the klunkers right away, so the group does not go over them again. (If the group can't decide if something is a klunker or not, it is not. Klunkers are obvious.)

STEP 3.   Then the editors makes editorial suggestions.

Suppose the editors decide to tell the author that the high point needs more suspense. Do they say, "Make the high point more suspenseful"? No. They say, "I think your high point needs more suspense. Remember that paragraph right before the train moved through the tunnel — the one where the dog was walking along the train tracks? Maybe you could stretch that out just a little longer and make us worry a little more about what will happen when the train comes through the tunnel."

When you are an editor, remember that you really need to think hard about your suggestions. Be specific. Give the author your best ideas, then let the author decide what to do.

STEP 4.   The author looks at the editors suggestions, decides what to do, and makes the revisions.

The last step on the loop is for the author to make changes to the piece. The group can wait for the author to make the changes before going around the loop with another editorial question or the group can go around the loop several times before the author revises.

Try following these rules when revising your work: Always work from big to little. Work on whole sections first, paragraphs next, then sentences, and finally individual words. When you revise, you can cut, rearrange, add, or rewrite. Try doing them in this order:

1. *Cut first.* When you cut out unnecessary sections, paragraphs, sentences, or words, you clear away everything that might cover up the good parts of your story. It's just like a gardener pulling weeds and trimming away dead branches in order to show off the pretty flowers.

2. *Rearrange second.* Once you have the weeds cleared out, you can see your story better. You can rearrange the order of the paragraphs into a clearer design. Use a pair of scissors and a roll of tape to cut the draft apart and rearrange the order.

3. *Add third.* Add any improvements you think would help your newly rearranged draft.

4. *Rewrite last.* Rewrite any sentences or paragraphs that you think need it.

BASIC EDITORIAL QUESTIONS (HANDOUT)

To help editors think of specific ideas, these editorial questions are arranged with an editorial question and follow-up questions that are more specific.

Nonfiction

1. What is the best part? Why?

2. Does the piece suit the ideal reader? Is the information appropriate to that ideal reader? Is there anything missing that the ideal reader would probably like to learn?

3. How does the mood add to the piece? Did the author maintain the same mood all the way through? Are there any sections where the mood is inconsistent?

4. Does the author say what he wants to say? What is the key idea? Does that key idea come across loud and clear?

5. What is the most interesting piece of information in the piece? How was it presented? Was it presented in the right place?

6. Did the writer use examples or anecdotes? Did they make the piece more fun to read? Could the piece use more examples or another anecdote?

7. Where is the piece easiest to understand? Are there any places the piece is hard to understand? Why? What could the author do to make it clearer?

8. Are there any unnecessary parts of the piece? Why aren't they necessary? Could the author cut it? How would cutting it improve the piece?

9. Choose two of the following words to describe the piece and explain why you chose it.

crisp	informative	funny	relaxed
serious	compact	detailed	helpful
organized	well-researched	entertaining	original
clear	flowing	sparkling	musical

10. If you could suggest one change that the author make, what would it be? Why?

Fiction

1. What is the best part? Why?

2. Are the characters easy to picture? What makes each important character interesting? Are the things they do consistent with their personalities? Does the dialogue fit the characters?

3. Who is the most interesting character? Why?

4. Which scene turned out best? Why?

5. Was the story easy to follow? Was there anything that did not make sense? Why?

6. Is the story even? Were some scenes cut too short or others a bit too long? What could the author do to even the story out?

7. Was the ending satisfying? Did the author tie up all the loose ends or did you end up wondering what happened to some characters? What could the author do to tie up loose ends and/or make the ending more satisfying?

8. Where is the best action, description, dialogue, or introspection in the story? Are there any places where the story could use more of any of these?

9. Are there any unnecessary scenes, characters, or other parts of the story? Why aren't they necessary? How would cutting them improve the story?

10. Does the crisis or high point have enough suspense to hold the reader? If not, what could the author do to add a little more suspense?

11. Choose two of the following words to describe the piece and explain why you chose those two.

snappy	moody	action-packed	suspenseful
relaxed	thoughtful	sparkling	musical
flowing	intriguing	well-plotted	inspiring
entertaining	funny	well-researched	serious

12. If you could suggest one change that the author make, what would it be?

Teacher's Notebook: On Grading Papers

As every writing teacher knows, grades and writing don't mix. Grades do everything good editors should not. Good editors are specific; grades aren't. Good editors help the writer finish; grades don't. Good editors don't act like critics; grades do. Grades teach students to measure their work against the opinion of just one person—something writers should never do. It is difficult to conceive of a worse editorial system than the traditional mark and grade. Still, students, parents, and school administrators expect grades. The trick is to find a grading method that doesn't violate the principles of good editing. Whatever method you use, think it through carefully and try to use these general principles:

1. Establish very clear standards in advance.

    Teachers vary wildly in the standards they emphasize. Some stress structure and content while others want every footnote properly formatted. Without clear written standards, students ping-pong from teacher to teacher guessing from a thousand possibilities what any particular teacher believes important.

    You need not mention whether you stress content, organization, or imagination. We simply list the number of practice pieces and portfolio pieces a student must complete in a term to receive an A, B, or C. We don't care about the quality of the practice pieces as long as students make a real effort. When students turn in work that is not ready for publishing approval, we write down a very specific list of the things they must do before they will receive approval.

2. Always provide students the opportunity to raise a grade by editing.

    Students do not have much incentive to edit under the traditional method of marking the paper with comments and turning it back with a grade. Many don't even read the comments. Why should they? Always give students a chance to read the comments and edit in order to raise the grade.

    Under our system students who fall short of the number of pieces for the grade they wish can always do more practice pieces or edit a piece to a portfolio standard.

3. Never give a grade on a specific paper—either good or bad—without explaining why.

    If students don't know why they received an A instead of a C, or vice versa, they will guess why. Their reasons can range from getting an A because they wrote precisely 284 words to getting a C because they did not use enough commas. These wrong guesses are extremely damaging in the long run. The next time, they will add padding or throw in a thousand extra commas at random in hope of success. Learning to write by this lottery method is neither efficient nor fair.

4. Never stress one set of standards in the assignment and another in the grading.

    Of course, it is obvious that teachers should not stress the content of the writing in the assignment and then mark down on spelling or manuscript preparation alone (although some inexperienced teachers do fall into this trap at first), but it is easy to do it by accident. Just marking all the spelling errors and then giving the grade on content can leave a student with a misunderstanding. Do not mark spelling or format errors if the grade stresses content. On a comment sheet, write something along the lines of "this assignment didn't count spelling, but you need to work on spelling."

5. Try to grade over several assignments.

    Most professionals throw away perhaps one of every three pieces. It's difficult to make a given piece turn out. Students work under tight deadlines and do not always have the time to try again. Give grades over several assignments and give students the option of throwing out at least one piece with which they are dissatisfied. (In our system, students don't need to worry about flops. They can count them as practice pieces and work on the pieces that did turn out.)

6. Never establish a fixed percentage of a grade for spelling or presentation.

    Students who have penmanship problems or difficulty spelling cannot correct the problem overnight. If spelling or penmanship counts as a fixed percentage of all grades, all of these students' work will be permanently marked down. They soon become discouraged with writing altogether.

7. Do your own assignments.

    If you want students to try a specific genre or technique, to write on a particular subject, or to cover certain major points, be sure to try writing your own assignment. The more detailed the requirements, the more important this is. We have seen countless writing assignments with such conflicting requirements that few people could write such a piece. Science, social studies, and English teachers assigning literary criticism should be especially careful. Take a look at the prewriting choices implied by the assignment, and at least try to write several good openings that would lead into such a piece. If you can't do it, your students probably won't be able to do it either.

8. Never mark up final copies.

    Teachers can't expect students to care about appearance of their work if their teachers constantly destroy the result by marking all over it. Even an "A—Good Job!" can be disappointing if it means retyping the first page in order to have a clean copy. Make a point of marking all your comments on a separate sheet of paper. Students appreciate teachers who show respect for their efforts.

POLISHING TO PUBLISH

Whereas experienced writers may not draw a sharp line between revision and polishing, beginners should. Revision is based on writing. It can be discussed with the same terms and goals as those used for planning and drafting. Polishing, on the other hand, encompasses a whole new world. There are several areas of polishing: polishing the style, correcting the mechanics of spelling and punctuation, and finally polishing the presentation. Behind each lies a whole field of complex decisions and rules. In order to discuss these decisions and rules, beginners first need to learn a whole new vocabulary, such as the parts of speech.

When students write using all the words they know and the complete range of sentences structures they use in speaking, they inevitably use words they can't yet spell and sentences they can't yet punctuate. If they confuse polishing with revision, they will also tend to confuse good writing with good polishing. Dead wrong. A piece can be perfectly spelled, correctly punctuated, beautifully presented, and horribly written. It can be beautifully written and horribly polished.

Take our advice. Take a break after revision, so students can build up their energies and see polishing as a separate project from writing. Never bring up polishing questions until students finish revising their work. Avoid mixing polishing questions in with revision questions when you comment or grade. Never try to teach new grammar, punctuation, or style rules through writing complete pieces or paragraphs. Students are too tired, and polishing a manuscript is a ludicrously slow way to learn a rule of punctuation or the spelling of a word. Teach mechanics separately. When you do teach mechanics, assign practice sentences, not paragraphs or stories. For example, never give assignments such as "write a story using the words on your spelling list." Change these assignments to "write ten sentences using the ten words on your spelling list."

When students do polish, keep in mind that part of their problem has nothing to do with their skills at mechanics. Writing takes as much endurance as it does talent or skill. That endurance is built by writing consistently every day over a long period of time. Writing is no different in this respect from sports that demand physical endurance. When beginners reach the polishing stage, many start to run out of steam. It isn't that they don't know how to correct the error or that they don't care. They are just too tired to do it. If you want students to do a careful job, break polishing into smaller stages and give them little breaks to rest up between stages.

Finally, although it is not always possible, we recommend asking students to polish only those pieces that they plan to publish. Polishing takes a good deal of time and energy. There really isn't any point in doing it if there isn't a reader on the other end. Most students really don't care that much if the teacher finds fault with the polishing. They do care if their ideal reader does. Polishing to publish puts the teacher in a better position to point out errors without discouraging the student as well. Students are glad to find the error and fix it it they are getting the piece ready to show off. Otherwise, they just think that polishing is nitpicking.

Polishing manuscripts *is* a good time to introduce students to the reference works that are the tools of the copyeditor's trade. Young students will not be able to use these books without help, but at the very least, they should know that such books exist. Youngsters assume that adults know all the rules by magic. It's a relief to discover that everybody needs to look them up—even professional copyeditors.

Keep one copy of the following books in the classroom and make a point of consulting them when students bring up questions:

A spelling dictionary: A small dictionary with spellings only; for example, *The New Century Vest-Pocket 50,000 Words.*

A misspeller's dictionary: A dictionary of commonly misspelled words organized by common misspellings; for example, *The Misspeller's Dictionary.*

A usage guide: We like Phyllis Martin's *Word Watcher's Handbook: A Deletionary of the Most Abused and Misused Words.*

A punctuation guide: We like Margaret Enright Wye's blessedly short *The Complete Guide to Punctuation: A Quick-Reference Deskbook.* We also like Barron's *The Art of Styling Sentences: 20 Patterns for Success* by Marie Waddell et al.—although it is a better teaching tool than a reference book.

A style guide: The most famous is Strunk and White's *The Elements of Style*, but there are many other good choices. Gary Provost's delightful *100 Ways to Improve Your Writing* contains an excellent collection of style tips. Finally, the most complete style manual around is *The Chicago Manual of Style* from the University of Chicago Press, a fascinating—if overwhelming—tour of the publishing process, from punctuation rules for writers who are preparing manuscripts to printer's typefaces. It should have a subtitle: "Everything you ever wanted to know about editing and more." It's worth keeping one copy in every school, so that students know that it exists and teachers have an authoritative guide to consult for tricky questions. Recently, some other presses, such as the *New York Times*, have published their style manuals in paperback. They are perhaps less complete than *The Chicago Manual*, but cheaper and less daunting.

The Chicago Manual is worth a special mention, however. Full of ideas for the creative teacher who wants to model the writing classroom on the publishing house, it has the most authoritative and intelligent explanation of punctuation and editing rules found anywhere. You can find a quick writing or editing lesson on days when you run short of activities by opening it to almost any page. By the time they leave high school, students should treat the book as they would a comfortable old shoe—taken for granted. If you can possibly spare the time, read it yourself, read it out loud to students, keep a beat up copy around the classroom along with a really good dictionary. Consult both often. Your students will thank you someday.

Activity 4:
Polishing for Style

It is not intentionally mannered writing that adds up to style,
or richly poetic paragraphs, or the frantic pursuit of novel
prose rhythms. The writer's own style emerges when he makes
no deliberate attempt to have any style at all.

—Lawrence Block

Don't ever ask students to follow particular style rules or imitate a style before they've finished drafting. Good style starts with writing simply and naturally in one's own style. The sound of a writer's own style, the natural voice, is as distinct as a singer's natural voice. There is a difference between singing operas in one's own voice and imitating an opera singer. The first may sound rough but honest; the second always sounds ridiculous. Writing styles are no different. Students should write in the natural voice. If they want to polish their style, the time to do it is during polishing.

Instructions for Students

Professional writers use some simple little tricks to perk up sentences. You can use them too. Follow these little tips, and your writing will really sound great.

STYLE TIPS (HANDOUT)

TIP #1:   Use the *active voice*, not the passive, most of the time.

Passive: The stories *were written by* the students.
Active: The students *wrote* stories.

Passive: The pen *was broken by* Sue.
Active: Sue *broke* the pen.

Passive: The experiment *was done by* the students in Group One.
Active: The students in Group One *did* the experiment.

To find the *passive voice*, look for "was _____ by" in the sentence. Change it to active by putting the subject of the sentence first.

TIP #2:   Replace abstract nouns with more concrete nouns.

Abstract: Beautiful *flowers* lined the path.
Specific: *Blue bachelor buttons and purple daisies* lined the path.

Abstract: A *dog* ran along the fence barking at *people*.
Specific: A *German shepherd* ran along the fence barking at *joggers*.

(Don't overdo it. Use your judgment.)

TIP #3:   Use simple, specific verbs that say two things at once.

General: She *was sitting* in the car.
More specific: She *waited* in the car.
                She sulked in the car.
                She *slept* in the car.

General: He *went across* the room.
More specific: He *marched* to the cupboard.
                He *slipped* across to the window.
                He *danced* across the room.

TIP #4:   "As" is a difficult word, especially in fiction. When you have used "as" in the middle of a sentence, try breaking the sentence into two sentences and reversing them.

One sentence:	I don't want to do this anymore, thought Sue as she tied another bow on another bouquet.
Two sentences, reversed:	Sue tied another bow on another bouquet. I don't want to do this anymore, she thought.

One sentence:	Jo wondered what the weather would be like when she got off the plane tomorrow as the thunder cracked outside and the first drops of the storm rattled on the window.
Two sentences, reversed:	The thunder cracked outside and the first drops of the storm rattled on the window. Jo wondered what the weather would be like when she got off the plane tomorrow.

TIP #5: Once is enough. If you've said something twice, cut out the weaker one.

Twice:	John walked across the kitchen and yanked open the refrigerator door. As he opened the refrigerator, a mouse ran out from under it.
Once:	John walked across the kitchen and yanked open the refrigerator door. A mouse ran out from under it.

Twice:	Hannibal led his men across the Alps and onto the plains of northern Italy. As they crossed the Alps, they fought snow and blinding hail and talked of victory once they reached the warm plains.
Once:	As Hannibal's men crossed the Alps, they fought snow and blinding hail and talked of a victory ahead on the warm plains of northern Italy.

TIP #6: Replace long, dull words with short punchy ones.

He demonstrated his happiness.

He smiled.

TIP #7: Cross out unnecessary adverbs. Look for every word ending in "ly" and ask yourself if you need it. If not, cross it out. "She shouted" or "it was awesome" are better than "she shouted loudly" and "it was totally awesome."

TIP #8: Take out useless clutter words if possible:

a little	very	really
sort of	too	mostly
kind of	pretty much	
rather	quite	

(Handout continues on page 142.)

TIP #9:   *THE BIG RULE*. Read every sentence out loud. Does it say something? Does it make sense? Does it sound clear and simple? Does it fit the mood of the writing? If not, rewrite it.

Some Style Tips That Don't Work

BAD TIP #1:   "Put commas where you take a breath." Singers spend years learning where and how to breathe. So do writers. Expert writers, who know all the rules of punctuation and proper breathing, can use this rule. If *you* try it, you may end up sprinkling commas everywhere sounding like you have a bad cold. Learn the rules of punctuation and use as few commas as possible.

BAD TIP #2:   "Don't repeat words." This is nonsense. Good writers repeat words all the time. If you change every repeated word to another, you'll sound like a sportscaster. By all means, don't pound your reader to death repeating words. But a little repetition for rhythm and emphasis is fine.

Activity 5:
Polishing for Pride

Word carpentry is like any other kind of carpentry.
You must join your sentences smoothly.

—Anatole France

Like all writers, students, too, suffer from manuscript blindness. Once a writer has reread a manuscript a certain number of times, even obvious errors become invisible.* For this reason, be sure that students help each other with spelling and punctuation.

Set up a very clear process. Include a procedure for checking the spelling and a list of punctuation rules to check. This type of detailed polishing can go on forever, so it sometimes helps students to set a time limit.

You can emphasize copyediting as much or as little as you wish, but don't overdo it. It's better to save the time for separate spelling and punctuation lessons than to waste it churning through manuscripts trying to find errors.

---

*Teachers suffer from a special version of manuscript blindness. They see so many misspellings and punctuation errors in student work that their own spelling and punctuation deteriorates. The worst copyeditor in the world may be a language arts teacher in the month of May.

Instructions to Students

You have all finished polishing the style in your work. Now we come to the next phase of polishing—copyediting. In publishing houses, copyediting also includes some style questions, facts checking, and other things. For school think of copyediting as checking the spelling and punctuation.

Look at it this way. Leaving spelling errors or sloppy punctuation in your work is like writing a play, then sitting in the audience playing a kazoo while people are trying to watch it. Everybody will forget the play and watch the kazoo. The same thing happens with stories. Everybody forgets the story and notices the misspelled word. If you want people to notice all your hard work, you must copyedit.

We're going to let you in a big secret: it's very hard for the author to copyedit his or her own work. There are two reasons. First, no one knows how to spell all 600,000 English words, and no one can remember all the rules of punctuation. The author who does not know how to spell a particular word often won't realize that it is misspelled until someone else points it out. Second, the author often has a little problem called "manuscript blindness." Your brain is a fantastic thing. It remembers what you *meant* to write down, even if you did not actually write it down that way. As you reread your own story, your brain fills in the missing words or rearranges the letters, and you don't even notice. After working so long, the author sometimes cannot see the simplest error.

What do you think is the secret to polishing? *Find someone to help you.* Two heads are better than one. It does not matter that you know how to spell everything or all the rules of punctuation. It *does* matter that you care enough to get help. In publishing houses, the special editors, called *copyeditors*, help writers polish these details. In our class your writing groups will also serve as copyeditors.

Today, you are going to copyedit your stories. Check the spelling first, then the punctuation. We have written the rules of punctuation that we want you to check on the blackboard. If you have any questions, make an appointment to ask a teacher.

We have two handouts to help you. The first shows you the steps for checking the spelling. The second, the personality of punctuation, is just for fun. It should give you some ideas for punctuation questions to check beyond the ones on the blackboard.

(Text continues on page 148.)

HOW TO CHECK SPELLING
(POLISHING HANDOUT #1)

STEP 1:   Mark the words.

Authors give their stories to their copyeditors. The copyeditor first reads through the piece and marks every word with questionable spelling. Don't correct the spelling. Just mark it. (Use a bright-colored pen or a highlighter marker. Blue or black pens are too hard to see.) The copyeditor then gives the piece to another person, either the author or another copyeditor. This second person also reads through the piece marking every questionable spelling that the first person may have missed. Once the piece is marked, it's returned to the author.

STEP 2:   Make a list.

The author makes a list of all the marked words on a separate sheet of paper.

STEP 3:   Check the list.

Using either a regular dictionary, a spelling dictionary, or a misspeller's dictionary, the author looks up every word on the list and writes down the correct spelling next to the original spelling.

STEP 4:   Correct the spelling.

The author looks at every marked word in the piece, crosses it out, and copies in the correct spelling over the misspelled word.

STEP 5:   List your "Dirty Dozen."

Each of you should choose twelve words from the list of words misspelled in your manuscript. These twelve words are your "Dirty Dozen." Copy down the correct spellings on a separate sheet of paper and save it. Practice spelling your dirty dozen. Keep your dirty dozen list at hand when you write, so you can easily check the words that give you the most trouble.

THE PERSONALITY OF PUNCTUATION
(POLISHING HANDOUT #2)

punctuation is not something that you must use because somebody made up some dumb rules and said that you gotta use them punctuation is part of your writing it helps your reader understand what you are saying when you speak you put in punctuation by pausing or by changing the way you say something but you cant do that when you write the only way to make your reader understand is to put in some punctuation stories without punctuation are very very very hard to read as you can see

Instead of thinking of punctuation as rules, try thinking of each piece of punctuation as a person who helps your reader.

Good old Joe, the period

When do you need Joe, the period? At the end of a sentence. Listen to your sentences as you read aloud. When you reach the end of a sentence (you can *hear* it), put in the period. Start the next sentence with a capital letter. Good old Joe is always around. He is relaxed, and he keeps your reader from feeling frantic, breathless, confused, and all strung together.

Jeeves, the comma

Jeeves, the comma, is an excellent butler — the kind you miss when he isn't there but hardly notice when he is. He performs many duties. He puts a very little pause in the sentence to separate words, phrases, or clauses. In fact, Jeeves is so quiet, yet so busy, that it takes quite awhile to learn when to use the comma. Below are some sample sentences to give you some ideas:

Punch, the puppet, is famous in England.

"Punch the puppet!" chanted the crowd.

That's a pretty small rabbit.

That's a pretty, small rabbit.

Whatever happens, happens because of you.

John, who is interested in jazz, bought concert tickets.

The old house, clearly not used for many years, was the gang's favorite hideout.

Jane and Bob, puffing and groaning, finally reached the top of the hill.

Why, Lindy, did you mail the letter without a stamp?

Why Lindy! What a surprise to see you.

They bought baseball bats, balls, and uniforms.

That quilt is black, white, and green.

Did you bring soda pop, potato chips, or hot dogs?

(Handout continues on page 146.)

All we ever do is punctuate, punctuate, punctuate!

The dog howled, and the cat meowed.

The dog howled, the cat meowed, and the mouse squeaked.

After the dog howled, the cat meowed.

If the dog howled, the cat meowed.

Since the dog howled, the cat has meowed, and a mouse squeaked.

Because the dog howled, the cat meowed.

While the dog howled, the cat meowed, and the mouse squeaked.

The loudmouth question mark

The *rule* is to put a question mark at the end of a question. The *truth* is that the question mark has a loud, irritating voice. Before you use the question mark, decide how loud you want the question to be. Use a period for soft, quiet questions.

Sally, the semicolon

Sally is shy, and most people don't get to know her, but Sally is very efficient and helpful—a good friend to writers. Sally can replace ", and" for connecting sentences.

She went to the door, and he went to the window, and the rest of us stayed put.

She went to the door; he went to the window; the rest of us stayed put.

The kibitzers, dashes and parentheses

When you use a phrase enclosed by dashes or parentheses, picture one of the people in the piece stopping the action, turning to the audience, and explaining something. The dash is briefer, less of a break than the parenthesis. You can use commas to pause instead of dashes. Be careful (sometimes these pauses are about as welcome as a backseat driver) with dashes and parentheses. Use them only when you want a break in the action.

It was a beautiful day, we all thought, for a softball game.

It was a beautiful day—we all thought—for a softball game.

It was a beautiful day (we all thought) for a softball game.

The interrupter, the ...

If a character is speaking and is interrupted, you write ... The "..." is called an *ellipses*. It indicates an interruption, a speech trailing off, or missing words.

"Billy Jo, I got that goat out of the garage. It ..."

"What goat?" Billy Jo asked. "Why would somebody keep a goat in the garage?"

Marallee put her foot in the stirrup and vaulted onto the horse. "Not bad for an amateur," she thought. "This is fun. I wonder how long George is going to take to ... Gosh, this horse is big."

Now, the interrupter can be extremely irritating. Use the ellipses (...) only when you don't mind your reader feeling just a little irritated at the interruption.

!, the BOMB!!!

If the world just blew up, use the exclamation point. Otherwise, avoid it. Beginners always use too many!!!!!!

The world blew up!

The world almost blew up.

The world could blow up?

:, the drill sergeant

The colon helps you get to the point fast. When you bring on the colon, your reader stands and salutes.

There are three colors of shoes on that shelf: purple, green, and pink.

Buy all of the school supplies on the list below:

There is a reason I never use colons: I always forget the rules.

If you are going camping don't forget the essentials: food, warm clothing, and a good book.

Remember, drill sergeants wear people out, so don't wear your reader out with too many colons. For example, the punctuation is correct in all the sentences below. But the colon really stops the action. The ! stops it too, but not as much. The dash and the comma stop it even less. Use the colon only when you want abrupt halts.

Hey you: the one with the purple tennis shoes.

Hey you! The one with the purple tennis shoes.

Hey you—the one with the purple tennis shoes.

Hey you, the one with the purple tennis shoes.

Activity 6:
Presentation Checklist

I love being a writer. What I can't stand is the paperwork.
—Peter De Vries

Some students have strong production values. They have a good sense of design, they like an attractive presentation, and they care about how the finished piece looks. These students are always tempted to skip editing and to start retyping and tidying up too soon. To others the presentation is about as important as a dust bunny under the sofa. Who cares how it looks if it sounds good? For these students production is a boring, but necessary chore. They'd much rather be writing. Still, presentation is an important part of writing. It should be the last thing students do, however. Book designers in publishing houses don't begin work until the copyeditors are finished, with good cause. Presentation takes a great deal of time all by itself. Making changes after something is typed always triples the effort.

Because recopying or typing take so much time and energy, students sometimes wear out before they finish. Parents can help with typing, but be sure to let them know that you don't object. Offering typing services every so often for special pieces relieves students of some of the burden. Typing teachers are sometimes willing to use student pieces as a class project for the typing class. Asking students to illustrate their pieces provides a little extra motivation for yet another long writing chore. Use the little presentation checkoff list on p. 149 to help students think through some of their presentation decisions.

Instructions to Students

Congratulations to all of you. You are almost finished writing. Sharing your stories with readers is what writing is all about, but you can't share until you finish. Readers can't enjoy your stories until the story is neatly recopied or typed. Messy stories are just awful to read. It's like watching a broken television. The picture always gets fuzzy at the best part. The last step of editing is presentation. It includes anything that you do to make your piece neat, attractive, and easy to read.

Before you start, you need to consider where your story will be published. If you are submitting stories to teachers or to writing contests, you need to present your story in manuscript form. Manuscripts are plain. They are neatly handwritten, printed, or typed. They are double-spaced and printed on one side of the page.

The other form of presentation is to make a galley. Use galleys when your piece will be displayed just as you produce it. The galley can be set up in any way you think would be attractive. You can illustrate it with drawings, use different type for titles and text, and you can print on both sides of the paper to make a booklet if you wish. You can single-space, mix typed sections with hand-printed sections, and anything else you think would show off your work at its best.

Whether you plan a manuscript or a galley, presentation is a lot of work. It's best to think it through before you begin. The "Presentation Checklist" we've passed out will help you make some of your decisions. We've left a space at the bottom for you to write any additional notes.

When you retype or recopy, you may make an error. Professional writers call them *typos*, and they hate them because typos are so hard to spot. Always ask one of your editors to read your final copy, marking typos in light pencil, so that you can fix them.

Please note: Once you give your story to other people, think about what would happen if someone dropped it. Would someone besides you be able to put the pages back together in order? Get into the habit of numbering every page. If the person to whom you will give your piece handles many stories, for instance, a teacher or a magazine editor, put your last name on every page as well.

PRESENTATION CHECKLIST (HANDOUT)

My piece will be (check the appropriate line)

1. Produced as a ＿＿＿＿＿＿ manuscript

    ＿＿＿＿＿＿ as a galley

2. Neatly handwritten in ＿＿＿＿＿＿ longhand

    ＿＿＿＿＿＿ print

3. Typed ＿＿＿＿＿＿ on a typewriter

    ＿＿＿＿＿＿ on a word processor

4. Written or typed ＿＿＿＿＿＿ Double-spaced

    ＿＿＿＿＿＿ Single-spaced (galleys only)

5. Written or typed ＿＿＿＿＿＿ on one side of the page

    ＿＿＿＿＿＿ on both sides (galleys only)

6. Will have illustrations ＿＿＿＿＿＿ yes (galleys only)

7. The title will be ＿＿＿＿＿＿ all capital letters

    ＿＿＿＿＿＿ mixed capital and small letters

8. The title will be ＿＿＿＿＿＿ centered

    ＿＿＿＿＿＿ flush left

9. The first line of a new paragraph will be ＿＿＿＿＿＿on a new line and set in five spaces

    ＿＿＿＿＿＿dropped two lines down and not set in

10. The page number will be ＿＿＿＿＿＿ at the bottom in the center

    ＿＿＿＿＿＿ at the bottom on the right

11. My full name will be written ＿＿＿＿＿＿ on a title page

    ＿＿＿＿＿＿ on the top of page 1

12. My last name will be written on the bottom left-hand corner of every page ＿＿＿＿＿＿ .

＿＿＿＿＿＿＿＿＿＿＿＿＿＿＿＿＿＿＿＿＿＿＿＿＿＿＿＿＿＿

＿＿＿＿＿＿＿＿＿＿＿＿＿＿＿＿＿＿＿＿＿＿＿＿＿＿＿＿＿＿

＿＿＿＿＿＿＿＿＿＿＿＿＿＿＿＿＿＿＿＿＿＿＿＿＿＿＿＿＿＿

＿＿＿＿＿＿＿＿＿＿＿＿＿＿＿＿＿＿＿＿＿＿＿＿＿＿＿＿＿＿

Activity 7:
The Publishing Game

For several days after my first book was published I carried it about in my pocket, and took surreptitious peeps at it to make sure the ink had not faded.

—James M. Barrie

Instructions to Students

For the next three weeks you are going to become part of a magazine publishing firm. This firm needs help getting reestablished. We have been losing subscriptions and we are at a loss as to what to do.

As members of the magazine staff, you will form teams of six to eight people. In the next three weeks each team will present the class with a magazine which you feel will bring the firm out of this slump.

I. Team Staff Members
    Each team will elect the following staff members for the publication (see job descriptions below).

    Writers

    Biography Editor

    Art Editor

    Format Editor

    Promotion Editor

II. Theme
    As a group discuss the idea of a theme for your magazine. *Examples:* News, Fashion, Holidays, Sports, Hobby, Special Audience, Science, Technical.

    After your theme is chosen, do the following:

    1. Design the cover and choose a title.
    2. Have your cover laminated.

III. Format
     Decide on the format or order of events and articles that will be in your magazine. The following items should be included in your magazine.

     1. Cover (designed front and back)
     2. Title
     3. Copyright page (contains publication date, name of publisher, and date to appear on newsstand)
     4. Pages numbered
     5. Table of contents (list all written items with their titles)

IV. Contents
Make a list of the types of articles, stories, and advertisements the magazine will contain. Below is a list of suggestions. Each magazine should have ten to twelve pieces. There can be more than one of the same type, but there should be several types.

Short stories

Poetry

National interest stories

International interest stories

Sports items

Book reviews

Contributor's page

Movie reviews

Syndicated column

How-to articles

Cartoons

Commercial advertisements

Your choice of any other ideas

V. Organization

The group will assign pieces to the writers and choose a deadline for submitting polished drafts.

As each piece of writing is finished, the format editor should look over the item. It should be proofread for any errors in form, punctuation, spelling, and grammar. The format editor gives publishing approval.

As soon as the material is passed for publishing, the writers will copy the pieces in pen or type, the art editor will complete the artwork, and the group will compile its magazine.

All the materials needed for construction can be found on the front table.

VI. Promotion
Once the magazine is ready, it is time for the promotion editor to prepare a promotion idea and present the team's magazine to the class for sale.

Job Description: Writers

Writers are responsible for the written portion of the magazine. Each writer may be assigned to write any number of articles, some of which the team may decide not to use. Writers can use pieces from their portfolio folder. They should also choose pictures or draw their own to illustrate the story and make it more interesting. Writers may want to read magazine articles to give them different ideas and styles for stories.

Job Description: Biography Editor

The biography editor interviews the writers, poets, and editors on the team to find out their home-towns and main interests, previous publications, and facts about their personal lives and writes a forty- to fifty-word "Contributor's Note" for each member on the team. (Note: Writers can "make up" their backgrounds.)

EXAMPLE

John Doe is a contributing editor to _____(name of magazine)_____ . His stories have appeared in *Mud* magazine and in *Scholastick Scope*. His latest venture is the founding of a new journal on the popular arts, *The Coyote Review*. John is a bachelor and lives in Yuma, Arizona, with his pet beagle, Lucky.

Job Description: Art Editor

The art editor will be in charge of all the pictures and artwork in the magazine. He or she will place the art on the page, and do any lettering necessary. The art editor can cut and paste artwork from the magazines brought by the team, use the Print Shop™ computer program, or draw the artwork. Remember, a neat magazine will sell better.

Job Description: Format Editor

The format editor is the quarterback of the team! It's up to the format editor to decide how the various parts of the magazine will be put together and to give publishing approval to incoming pieces. Find out from all other staff members what articles they are working on, then make a list of the titles and lengths. Make sure everyone does his or her job.

Specific jobs:

1. Make a table of contents of all articles, poems, and stories for the magazine. Assign page numbers to each entry.

2. Next, make a copyright page for the magazine using one from a book or magazine as an example. Be sure to include the facts of publication, the name of the company, and the date.

3. Proofread all the work turned in. Correct grammar, spelling, and other errors. (Writers who finish early should help with this job.)

Job Description: Promotion Editor

The promotion editor will create a three-minute speech calculated to "sell" the team's magazine to potential buyers (students in other classes?).

Tips:

1. Make the talk as persuasive as possible, explaining why this is a good magazine to buy and giving the audience some idea of the interesting articles it contains. Consider the strong points of the publication and the kinds of people who may want to buy it—the magazine's ideal readers.

2. Find out specific information, such as (a) titles and writers for each story, poem, and article, (b) title and price of the magazine, and (c) biographical information about the writers and editors on the staff. (See the biography editor.)

3. Write a rough draft and practice the talk in front of other members of the team.

4. When the magazine is put together, deliver the talk before the entire group with enthusiasm!

5. As an added gimmick, make sample order forms. Mention them in the talk in order to sell subscriptions.

Teacher's Notebook: On Writing and Spelling

Curiously, spelling poses a particular problem for writers. The English language with its huge vocabulary and flexibility is one of the most beautiful languages for writing, but its spelling is a mess. In English, the sound of words is not consistently connected with the spelling, nor do any rules consistently apply. Despite numerous attempts at spelling reform and a thousand efforts to teach this hodge-podge "scientifically," the only way to learn to spell an English word is to memorize how it looks, ignoring for the most part how it sounds.

Spelling favors people who remember how words look (visual memory). It penalizes those who remember how they sound (auditory memory). The best spellers are those with good visual memory and poor auditory memory. The next best are those with good visual memory and good auditory memory. Worst of all are those poor souls with a good auditory memory but poor visual memory: they'll be labeled as "bad spellers" all of their lives.

Drafting, by contrast, favors auditory memory. Writing is like singing. Remembering the sound and the flow of words helps writers draft realistic dialogue, write musical description and metaphors, and structure fluent sentences. Unfortunately, those with great natural talent for writing are often poor spellers. Mark Twain is a classic example. He couldn't spell his way off the Mississippi, yet his ear for American English was so acute that he laid the foundation for American literature the day *Huckleberry Finn* was published.

Young students, who are learning to spell as they learn to write, have a dangerous tendency to confuse good spelling with good writing. If they struggle with spelling, they may conclude that they cannot write and give it up. Be especially careful with young students or those with spelling problems to praise the writing before mentioning spelling problems. Avoid mixing comments on the writing with spelling corrections. Never downgrade a piece because of the spelling. Help students correct the spelling and use rough drafts to make lists of the words that give them the most trouble for later practice (see the "Dirty Dozen," p. 144). Working on troublesome words a few at a time is the easiest way to improve spelling.

Teacher's Notebook: On
Simple Ways to Publish

Teacher often dread publishing because it can become a time-consuming hassle. Publishing is the fun part for students. It's disappointing to put in so much effort if there is no payoff, so try to keep a list of simple publishing techniques handy. You can save yourself a great deal of effort if you don't try to publish en masse. Collect student work in their portfolios and then publish a few students at a time. Here's a list of suggestions:

1. Day to day publishing. Our standard publishing method is to display copies of student work, along with a biography and a picture, on the "Authors of the Week" bulletin board. It's quick and simple. Students enjoy looking over the work of students who published that week, and each student who does publish gets a little more attention. Another quick method of publishing is to have students read their work at a "reading" before the class, a school assembly, or a lunchtime gathering. Don't forget the morning announcements over the school intercom for poetry and fillers. Finally, the student anthology is always popular with students because they get to be part of a book. Select ten to fifteen students who have pieces ready, and ask them to draw the cover, illustrations, and the table of contents. Then make a photocopy of the anthology for each student.

2. *Recordings.* Students can record their stories on tape (complete with sound effects, if they wish) or on videotape. Publish them by lending the tapes to a local nursing home, libraries for the blind and handicapped, or the local children's hospital. Sometimes public radio stations are willing to help students record and broadcast the work, as are the public access divisions of local cable networks.

3. *School exchanges.* Middle and high school students enjoy sharing their stories with younger students either through readings or tapes. One of our favorite projects is to have students chose a particular elementary or middle school student as an ideal reader, write a story especially for that student, and personally read the story to their ideal readers. School writing clubs can exchange tapes or hold joint readings.

4. *Letters.* Letters are an excellent way to publish because students are likely to get a response. Politicians are always good about responding, and students enjoy expressing their opinions on subjects of interest. In our experience, students writing to their favorite author often get warm, encouraging letters in return. Many children's authors make a point of personally responding to every child who writes.

5. *Contests.* Writing contests are always good places to submit student work, but students should be aware that most contests receive hundreds, if not thousands, of entries. It does not mean they are poor writers if they don't win. It just means that they have a lot of competition. (Be sure students follow the contest rules.)

   The Writer's Market publishes a list of nationwide contests and keeps the list updated in its monthly issues. The best contests, however, are usually local. Check with local civic clubs and citizens groups. Those that don't sponsor a contest already might be persuaded to do so. For example, the Puget Sound Chapter of the L-5 Society, a citizens group interested in space exploration, was persuaded by one writer to sponsor a contest for students writing about space. The contest was judged by a local science fiction writer, and the prizewinners got to meet an astronaut. Keep a list of teachers in your district who are interested in contests. Sometimes the ready-made list of contacts will encourage groups to sponsor a contest. Look in the *Writer's Market* for the name of the local writers conference. Most sponsor a contest every year, and some have categories for student work. Ask the school writing club or the PTSA to sponsor a contest if they don't already. The awards do not need to be spectacular: a copy of a book by the winner's favorite author, a certificate, or ribbon will do.

6. *Publishers.* The *Writer's Market* and its companion *Fiction Writer's Market* are published by Writers Digest Books each fall. They list virtually every publisher in the country, along with what sorts of pieces each publisher wants. They also have articles on how to write query letters, prepare manuscripts, and other tips on publishing. They list the names of authors' agents, writing groups, and contests and awards.

In our experience, however, students have about as much chance of publishing through a commercial publisher as they have of being struck by lightning. Publishing houses routinely receive thousands of "over-the-transom" manuscripts. Most go in the wastebasket without a reply. Exceptional student work has a better chance of being published in local magazines, small magazines, education magazines, such as *Scholastic Scope*, and highly specialized magazines. For example, one of our students, whose main aim in life was to be a mechanic, wrote a piece about a day at the drag races. After a good deal of pushing to get the piece polished, we sent it to a drag-racing magazine on the off-chance. To our surprise, they accepted it. It was quite a thrill to receive recognition from people whose opinion he valued. But this is rare. Publishing a regular school magazine is just about as much work and may be a better option in the long run.

7. *The School Writing Club.* In every school there are students who are crazy about writing. They need a writing club, so that they can meet others who share their interest. The writing club can sponsor visiting authors, organize readings, run contests, put out a magazine, or whatever they wish. Just the chance to share their stories with other interested students is a great opportunity for them, and they, in turn, heighten the visibility of writing in the whole school. If they are looking for a motto, we ran across a dandy one the other day:

Outside of a dog, books are man's best friend.
Inside of a dog, it's too dark to read.
—Groucho Marx

Bibliography

Adelman, Robert H. *What's Really Involved in Writing and Selling Your Book*. Los Angeles: Nash Publishing, 1972.

Asimov, Isaac. *Book of Facts*. New York: Grosset and Dunlap, 1979.

_____. *Fantastic Voyage*. Boston: Houghton Mifflin Co., 1966.

_____. *I, Robot*. New York: Ballantine Books, 1983.

Baker, Samm Sinclair. *Writing Nonfiction That Sells*. Cincinnati, Ohio: Writer's Digest Books, 1986.

Bartlett, John. *Familiar Quotations*. Secaucus, N.J.: Citadel Press, 1983.

Bates, Jefferson D. *Writing with Precision, How to Write So That You Cannot Possibly Be Misunderstood*. Washington, D.C.: Acropolis Books, 1983.

Bethancourt, T. Ernesto. *Dog Days of Arthur Cane*. New York: Holiday House, 1976.

Block, Lawrence. *Writing the Novel from Plot to Print (A Step-by-Step Guide from Idea to the Final Sale)*. Cincinnati, Ohio: Writer's Digest Books, 1986.

Bocca, Geoffrey. *You Can Write a Novel*. Englewood Cliffs, N.J.: Prentice-Hall, 1983.

Boeschen, John. *Freelance Writing for Profit: A Guide to Writing and Selling Nonfiction Articles*. New York: St. Martin's Press, 1982.

Boggess, Louise. *Article Techniques That Sell*. San Mateo, Calif.: B & B Press, 1978.

Boles, Paul Darcy. *Storycrafting*. Cincinnati, Ohio: Writer's Digest Books, 1984.

Bradbury, Ray. *The Veldt*. Mankato, Minn.: Creative Education, 1987.

Brande, Dorothea. *Becoming a Writer*. Los Angeles: J. P. Tarcher, 1981.

Bregonier, Reginald, and David Fisher. *What's What: A Visual Glossary of the Physical World.* New York: Ballantine Books, 1982.

Buzan, Tony. *Use Both Sides of Your Brain.* New York: E. P. Dutton, 1983.

Carroll, Lewis. *Alice in Wonderland.* New York: Putnam Publishing Group, 1986.

Charlton, James, ed. *The Writer's Quotation Book: A Literary Companion.* New York: Penguin Books, 1981.

Cheney, Theodore A. Rees. *Getting the Words Right: How to Revise, Edit & Rewrite.* Cincinnati, Ohio: Writer's Digest Books, 1984.

The Chicago Manual of Style: For Authors, Editors, and Copywriters. 13th ed. Chicago: University of Chicago Press, 1982.

Collins, Wilkie. *The Moonstone.* New York: Paperback Library, 1966.

Cook, Claire Kehrwald. *The MLA's Line by Line: How to Edit Your Own Writing.* Boston: Modern Language Association of America and Houghton Mifflin Co., 1985.

Cross, Peter R., ed. *Write a Teacher-Aid Book.* Belmont, Calif.: Fearon-Pitman Publishers, 1978.

Daniels, Harvey A. *Famous Last Words: The American Language Crisis Reconsidered.* Carbondale and Edwardsville, Ill.: Southern Illinois University Press, 1983.

Dean, John F. *Writing Well: 60 Simply-Super Lessons to Motivate and Improve Students' Writing.* Belmont, Calif.: David S. Lake Publishers, 1985.

Delton, Judy. *The Twenty-Nine Most Common Writing Mistakes and How to Avoid Them.* Cincinnati, Ohio: Writer's Digest Books, 1985.

Doyle, Michael, and David Straus. *How to Make Meetings Work: The New Interactive Method.* New York: Berkley Publishing Group, 1976.

Edwards, Betty. *Drawing on the Right Side of the Brain: A Course in Enhancing Creativity and Artistic Confidence.* Los Angeles: J. P. Tarcher, 1979.

Edwards, Charlotte. *Writing from the Inside Out.* Cincinnati, Ohio: Writer's Digest Books, 1984.

Elbow, Peter. *Writing with Power: Techniques for Mastering the Writing Process.* New York: Oxford University Press, 1981.

Ephron, Delia. *How to Eat Like a Child, and Other Lessons in Not Being a Grown-up.* New York: Viking-Penguin, 1978.

Evans, Bergen. *Dictionary of Quotations.* New York: Delacorte Press, 1968.

Fader, Daniel. *The New Hooked on Books, How to Learn and How to Teach Reading and Writing with Pleasure.* New York: Berkley Books, 1982.

Francis, Dick. *Flying Finish.* New York: Pocket Books, 1975.

_____. *The Racing Game (Odds Against).* New York: Pocket Books, 1984.

_____. *Reflex.* New York: Fawcett Crest, 1982.

Goldberg, Natalie. *Writing Down the Bones: Freeing the Writer Within.* Boston: Shambhala Publications, 1986.

Grahame, Kenneth. *The Wind in the Willows.* New York: Charles Scribner's Sons, 1960.

Graves, Donald H. *Writing: Teachers and Children at Work.* Portsmouth, N.H.: Heinemann Educational Books, 1983.

Griffith, Benjamin W. *A Pocket Guide to Literature and Language Terms.* Woodbury, N.Y.: Barron's Educational Series, 1986.

Herriot, James. *All Creatures Great and Small.* New York: St. Martin's Press, 1972.

_____. *The James Herriot's Dog Stories.* New York: St. Martin's Press, 1986.

Holt, John. *Freedom and Beyond.* New York: Dell Publishing Co., 1973.

_____. *The Underachieving School.* New York: Dell Publishing Co., 1970.

Hudson, Kenneth. *The Dictionary of Even More Diseased English.* Chicago: Academy Chicago, 1983.

Kane, Eileen. *Doing Your Own Research: How to Do Basic Descriptive Research in the Social Sciences and Humanities.* London: Marion Boyars, 1985.

Kendall, Carol. *The Gammage Cup.* San Diego, Calif.: Harcourt Brace Jovanovich, 1986.

Kennedy, X. J., and Dorothy M. Kennedy, eds. *The Bedford Reader.* Bedford, Tex.: Bedford Books, 1984.

Kipling, Rudyard. *Just So Stories.* New York: Macmillan, 1982.

Klauser, Henriette Anne. *Writing on Both Sides of the Brain: Breakthrough Techniques for People Who Write.* San Francisco: Harper & Row, 1986.

Knapp, Daniel, and John Dennis. *Writing for Real.* Englewood Cliffs, N.J.: Prentice-Hall, 1972.

Leavitt, Hart Day, and David A. Sohn. *Look, Think & Write, Using Pictures to Stimulate Thinking and Improve Your Writing.* Lincolnwood, Ill.: National Textbook Co., 1986.

LeGuin, Ursula K. *Rocannon's World.* New York: Ace Books, 1980.

Lewis, Norman. *Word Power Made Easy, the Complete Handbook for Building a Superior Vocabulary.* New York: Pocket Books, 1979.

London, Jack. *To Build a Fire.* Mankato, Minn.: Creative Education, 1980.

Macrorie, Ken. *Twenty Teachers.* New York: Oxford University Press, 1984.

Madsen, Sheila, and Bette Gould. *The Teacher's Book of Lists.* Santa Monica, Calif.: Goodyear Publishing Co., 1979.

Martin, Harold C. *The Logic & Rhetoric of Exposition.* New York: Rhinehart & Co., 1958.

Martin, Phyllis. *Word Watcher's Handbook: A Deletionary of the Most Abused and Misused Words.* New York: St. Martin's Press, 1982.

McCaffrey, Anne. *The Dragonriders of Pern.* New York: Ballantine Books, 1979.

McGinnis, Alan Loy. *Bringing Out the Best in People: How to Enjoy Helping Others Excel.* Minneapolis, Minn.: Augsburg Publishing House, 1985.

McManus, Patrick F. *A Fine and Pleasant Misery.* New York: Holt, Rinehart and Winston, 1978.

———. *Never Sniff a Gift Fish.* New York: Holt, Rinehart and Winston, 1983.

———. *They Shoot Canoes, Don't They?* New York: Holt, Rinehart and Winston, 1981.

Mencken, H. L. *The American Language.* New York: Alfred A. Knopf, 1986.

The Misspeller's Dictionary. New York: Simon and Schuster, 1983.

Morris, William, and Mary Morris. *Morris Dictionary of Word and Phrase Origins.* New York: Harper & Row, 1977.

Murray, Donald M. *A Writer Teaches Writing.* Boston: Houghton Mifflin Co., 1985.

The New American Desk Encyclopedia. New York: New American Library, 1984.

O. Henry. *The Ransom of Red Chief.* Mankato, Minn.: Creative Education, 1980.

Ohuigin, Sean. *Scary Poems for Rotten Kids.* Windsor, Ont.: Black Moss Press, 1983.

Owen, David. *None of the Above: Behind the Myth of Scholastic Aptitude.* Boston: Houghton Mifflin Co., 1985.

Pascal, Francine. *Hangin' Out with Cici.* New York: Dell, 1986.

Paterson, Katherine. *Bridge to Terabithia.* New York: Thomas Y. Crowell, 1977.

Paulsen, Gary. *Dogsong*. New York: Bradbury Press, 1985.

_____. *Mr. Tuckett*. New York: Funk and Wagnalls, 1969.

Peter, Laurence J. *Peter's Quotations: Ideas for Our Time*. New York: Bantam Books, 1980.

Phillips, Kathleen C., and Barbara Steiner. *Creative Writing: A Handbook for Teaching Young People*. Littleton, Colo.: Libraries Unlimited, 1985.

Polking, Kirk, Joan Bloss, and Colleen Cannon. *Writer's Encyclopedia*. Cincinnati, Ohio: Writer's Digest Books, 1986.

Provost, Gary. *100 Ways to Improve Your Writing*. New York: New American Library, 1985.

Rico, Gabriele Lusser. *Writing the Natural Way: Using Right-Brain Techniques to Release Your Expressive Powers*. Los Angeles: J. P. Tarcher, 1983.

Rockwell, F. A. *How to Write Plots That Sell*. Chicago: Contemporary Books, 1975.

Rodale, J. I. *The Synonym Finder*. Emmaus, Pa.: Rodale Press, 1978.

Ross-Larson, Bruce. *Edit Yourself: A Manual for Everyone Who Works with Words*. New York: W. W. Norton & Co., 1985.

Saling, Ann. *The Foundations of Fiction*. Edmonds, Wash.: Ansal Press, 1984.

Shute, Nevil. *The Far Country*. London: Pan Books, 1967.

Silverstein, Shel. *Where the Sidewalk Ends: Poems & Drawings*. New York: Harper & Row Junior Books, 1974.

Smart, William. *Eight Modern Essayists*. New York: St. Martin's Press, 1965.

Smith, Frank. "Reading Like a Writer." *Language Arts* 60, no. 5 (May 1983): 558-67.

Solzhenitsyn, Alexsandr I. *Gulag Archipelago, 1918-1956: An Experiment in Literary Investigation*. New York: Harper & Row, 1984.

Stahl, James, ed. *Merlyn's Pen*. East Greenwich, R.I.: Merlyn's Pen Inc.

Strunk, William, and E. B. White. *The Elements of Style*. New York: Macmillan, 1979.

Terhune, Albert Payson. *Lad: A Dog*. Cutchogue, N.Y.: Buccaneer Books, 1981.

Thomas, Lewis. *The Lives of a Cell: Notes of a Biology Watcher*. New York: Bantam Books, 1975.

Tolkien, J. R. R. *The Hobbit*. Boston: Houghton Mifflin Co., 1966.

Trager, James, ed. *The People's Chronology: A Year-by-Year Record of Human Events from Prehistory to the Present.* New York: Holt, Rinehart and Winston, 1979.

Tripp, Rhoda Thomas, ed. *The International Thesaurus of Quotations.* New York: Harper & Row, 1987.

Viorst, Judith. *If I Were in Charge of the World & Other Worries.* New York: Macmillan, 1981.

Waddell, Marie L., Robert M. Esch, and Roberta R. Walker. *The Art of Styling Sentences: 20 Patterns for Success: How to Write Sentences with Greater Clarity, Variety, and Style.* Woodbury, N.Y.: Barron's Educational Series, 1983.

Waldhorn, Arthur, Olga S. Weber, and Arthur Zeiger, eds. *Good Reading.* 22d ed. New York: New American Library, 1986.

Wallace, Irving. *The Book of Lists #2.* New York: William Morrow & Co., 1980.

Weisberg, Robert. *Creativity: Genius and Other Myths.* New York: W. H. Freeman and Co., 1986.

Whissen, Thomas. *A Way with Words: A Guide for Writers.* New York: Oxford University Press, 1982.

Winokur, Jon, ed. *Writers on Writing.* Philadelphia: Running Press, 1986.

Wonder, Jacquelyn, and Priscilla Donovan. *Whole-Brain Thinking: Working from Both Sides of the Brain to Achieve Peak Job Performance.* New York: William Morrow & Co., 1984.

The Writer. Boston: Writer Inc.

Writer's Digest Magazine. Cincinnati, Ohio: Fletcher Art Services.

Wye, Margaret Enright. *The Complete Guide to Punctuation: A Quick-Reference Deskbook.* New York: Prentice Hall Press, 1986.

The Yankee. Dublin, N.H.: Yankee, Inc.

Zavatsky, Bill, and Ron Padgett, eds. *The Whole Word Catalogue 2: A Unique Collection of Ideas and Materials to Stimulate Creativity in the Classroom.* New York: Teachers & Writers Collaborative (McGraw-Hill Paperbacks), 1977.

Zinsser, William. *On Writing Well: An Informal Guide to Writing Nonfiction.* New York: Harper & Row, 1985.

Index